STAND UP
AND

F   T

STAND UP
AND
FIGHT
BACK

KEN ABRAHAM

CHARISMA
HOUSE

STAND UP AND FIGHT BACK by Ken Abraham
Published by Charisma House
Charisma Media/Charisma House Book Group
600 Rinehart Road
Lake Mary, Florida 32746
www.charismahouse.com

Cover design by Justin Evans
Design Director: Bill Johnson

Visit the author's website at www.kenabrahambooks.com.

Some names and details of the stories have been changed, and any
similarity between the names and stories of individuals described in this
book to individuals known to readers is purely coincidental.

Library of Congress Cataloging-in-Publication Data:
An application to register this book for cataloging has been submitted to
the Library of Congress.
International Standard Book Number: 978-1-61638-964-2
E-book ISBN: 978-1-61638-965-9

While the author has made every effort to provide accurate telephone
numbers and Internet addresses at the time of publication, neither the
publisher nor the author assumes any responsibility for errors or for
changes that occur after publication.

This publication has been translated in Spanish under the title *Levántate y
lucha* , copyright © 2013 by Ken Abraham, published by Casa Creación, a
Charisma Media company. All rights reserved.

First edition

13 14 15 16 17 — 9 8 7 6 5 4 3 2 1
Printed in the United States of America

CONTENTS

ACKNOWLEDGMENTS

THE WRITING OF a book is always a collaborative process, and blessed is the author who has a good team of associates with whom he or she can work. I count myself in that number because the team at Charisma House and the friends and family surrounding me and upholding me in prayer as I have worked on this project have been above and beyond anything I could have imagined. I am deeply indebted to all.

I especially want to thank Michael Briggs, of Briggs Creative, who recognized the need for this book and initiated the process. I've known Mike longer than either of us cares to admit, and I value his judgment and insights regarding publishing. More importantly I cherish him as one of my finest friends. Thanks, Mike! With every person who finds help or inspiration from these pages, may you be greatly blessed, now and forevermore.

Special thanks also to Debbie Marrie and Adrienne Gaines of Charisma House for guiding me through the editorial process. I appreciate your spiritual understanding and your desire to produce a book that honors Jesus and is eminently readable and practical.

To my nephew, Brandon Bailey—who took an interest in this book from the beginning and helped keep me on track even when I didn't feel much like writing, checking on my progress, motivating me, and encouraging me to get it done—I am truly grateful. Thanks, Brandon! May this book help you to spiritually "stand up and fight back."

Chapter One

WE'RE IN FOR A FIGHT

I'M A LOVER, not a fighter. That's just the way my personality operates. I'm normally a calm, collected sort of person; I rarely lose my temper and don't get rattled easily. I'm the middle brother of three, so like most middle-born children, my role in the family is usually that of peacemaker. Through most of my high school years I worked hard to help people get along with one another. Even while in college during the turbulent sixties and seventies, I was more interested in building bridges between brothers and sisters than I was in blowing up buildings. Still today I don't go looking for fights and will avoid conflict as much as possible.

But when it comes to our spiritual lives, we don't have a choice. To be a Christian means that we are involved in a conflict, a spiritual war between God's people and the forces of Satan. As is the case in any war, we are affected whether we want to be or not.

We are at war with evil, a personal evil, a supernatural evil spearheaded by Satan himself. The devil is not some funny-looking cartoon character with horns sticking out of his head, dressed in red leotards, and carrying a pitchfork. No, the devil is real, and he is your enemy. He has sent his demonic messengers into the world to stand against you and do all they can to keep you from being the person God wants you to be.

The war is raging in cities and towns all across the land. The front is not confined to the major metropolitan areas, though the devil no doubt has dispatched large demonic regiments to those locations. Equally disruptive and destructive forces have invaded rural areas as well. Furthermore the battle is not restricted to what we might be tempted to refer to as "the devil's playground"—bars, adult bookstores, and sorcery shops. The war has moved inside the doors of governments, schools, churches, and homes.

Sadly Satan is winning victories on many fronts. He is bowling people over, knocking numerous kingpins in the kingdom of God right off the platform. The devil and his demonic cohorts are ripping apart friendships, marriages, and other family relationships. They are splitting churches wide open, sapping the lifeblood out of many believers, and sucking some your friends and family members right down into hell.

What are we going to do about it?

It is time to stand up and fight back! In the name of Jesus, by the power of His Holy Spirit working in us, and by the blood of the Lamb, it is time for each of us to tell the devil where to get off. God is calling us out of our complacency to become warriors for Christ. He wants us to learn how to put on the full armor of God, how to overcome the evil one, and to challenge the demonic powers that have captured so many of the world systems, our churches, our schools, friends, and family members.

It is going to be a fight to the finish, with life and death hanging in the balance. Heaven or hell is literally at stake. This is no party game. This is the real thing. This is war!

"Whoa! Whoa! Whoa!" I can almost hear you protest. "I didn't sign up for any war. I wasn't drafted, and I certainly didn't volunteer. I didn't trust Jesus as my Savior and Lord to get involved in a fight that I didn't pick. I came to Jesus to find the love, joy, and peace I heard He could give me. Everybody told me I could have 'satisfaction guaranteed' here on earth, and that I could go to heaven someday, a long time from now, when I die. *Nobody* said anything about fighting. And they sure didn't tell me I'd have to go to war!"

I empathize with you. When I first trusted Jesus, I thought I had signed on for an eternal party. "The Christian life is like one big celebration," my friends told me. They weren't lying or trying to deceive me. But, like me, they didn't understand that although the Christian life is filled with joy, peace, love, and praise to our God, the real party doesn't start until Jesus Christ returns and sets up His heavenly kingdom. Until that time, while we may enjoy occasional celebrations and respites, we will be perpetually at war.

Everyone who is born into the kingdom of God inherits the conflict that has been raging since before Adam and Eve sinned in the Garden of Eden. Consider this: the babies born during the Nazi bombardment of London in World War II didn't ask to become involved in war. They just woke up one morning, and bombs were blasting all around them. Buildings were crumbling. Fire and smoke filled the air. Sirens wailed. Death and destruction surrounded those precious newborn babies. Day after day, night after night, Hitler's planes droned in their eardrums, and then came the awful sounds of more bombs exploding in London's devastated business district.

The babies born during that time hadn't picked a fight with Hitler and his henchmen. The babies inherited a mortal enemy, and Hitler hated those British infants as much as he hated their parents.

In a similar way you have inherited a war against the devil and his demons. Adam and Eve left you that legacy, long before your parents even conceived you. The war is already on; the only question now is, will you stand up and fight back?

But I Don't Want to Fight

Most of us don't like to fight with the devil. That's smart. Only a fool would seek a confrontation with a supernatural, demonic being. Unfortunately that evil intruder has come looking for you, trying to rape, rob, and rip you off in every way possible. He does not fight fairly, and he does not wait for an invitation. Jesus called him a liar, a murderer, and a thief (John 8:44; 10:10). He is a bully and a bluffer. You can either defend yourself against him, learn to take authority over him, or sit back and watch him plunder and destroy your home, your family, and your future.

God has blessed me with a wonderful family, with three beautiful daughters and one incredibly gorgeous granddaughter (our first—couldn't you tell?). I love them dearly and would do anything for them. Even though I am not by nature a fighter, if I awoke in the middle of the night and discovered an assailant in their bedroom, you'd better believe that I would not be a peacemaker. I wouldn't be laid back, unruffled, or unconcerned. Nor would I think, "Well, I guess this intruder has a good reason to be in our house, invading our property. No doubt he has seen the love and joy shared by our beautiful family members and has come here to admire them or to bring them a present."

That would be ludicrous. I would be furious, and fighter or not, my fists would be flailing against anyone who even hinted he might be a threat to my family.

Yet too many of us simply view the satanic incursions into our governments, churches, schools, homes, or personal lives as something we must accept. Oh, no we don't. We need not put up with demonic oppression in the form of infirmities, demonically inspired sicknesses, depression, discouragement, certain kinds of persecution, and other difficulties brought on by the devil and his evil band. Granted, not every calamity that comes to a Christian is directly attributable to the devil. Nevertheless too many believers are allowing themselves to be beaten and battered by demonic opposition.

Many Christians don't really understand who Jesus is, who they are in Christ, or how Jesus defeated the devil by dying on the cross. Others wonder why they must fight if the devil has already been defeated. Consequently every time they get hit by demonic punches, they take another step backward and hope the demons will go away.

They won't.

Every time you step back from the devil's blows, count on it: you are going to get hit again. Probably harder. Demons are like flies; they swarm to the blood oozing from fresh wounds. They are like vultures, circling in the sky, waiting for the opportune time to swoop in for the kill. The only way to defeat the demonic forces opposing you is to stand up and fight back. When the enemy is in the bedroom, it is not enough to say, "Well, Jesus is already the victor; I'll just roll over and go back to sleep." You have to get up and fight.

PREPARE FOR WAR!

The church of Jesus Christ is not a country club. It is an army. Certainly, when you first come to know Christ, His church is a sanctuary for you, a place where you can love and be loved unconditionally. It's a hospital where you can find healing for the bumps and bruises you receive as you travel through life. But you must understand that the church is not a place to hide; it is where you get bandaged, refreshed, encouraged, and then sent back out to do battle with the enemy again.

Since the fall of Adam and Eve God has been getting His church ready for all-out war. Already many brave warriors who have blazed a trail before us have encountered fierce battles with the enemy. Undoubtedly in the days ahead we will experience some of the most intense spiritual warfare the world has ever known. We may see some victories for God in ways that were previously considered next to impossible, against forces that were thought to be impenetrable. Simultaneously we may see some of our worst setbacks ever.

Why? Because Satan knows that his time is limited. Jesus is coming back soon in final and ultimate victory. He broke the devil's power on Calvary's cross, and it is almost time for Him to cast the devil and his demons into their eternal place of torment. Until then the enemy is waging a last-ditch effort. Satan is pulling out all the stops. Now in addition to deceiving subtly, he is coming out in the open, entering into direct confrontation with members of Christ's kingdom. The devil is trying to destroy all that he can in these days. He will not stop until the entire world plunges into war, the final conflict, known in the Bible as the Battle of Armageddon.

Although we know Jesus is the victor now, and He will be then, until that time we must fight. Demonic influences have always been with us, but as we see the day of the final battle between the kingdom of God and the kingdom of evil approaching, we can expect an outpouring of satanic activity unlike anything the world has ever known. We have already seen the rise of the occult, open allegiance to Satan, a renewed interest in witchcraft, and the flourishing of mediums, seers, psychics, and fortune-tellers. We have stood by watching as false religions continue to gain strength and numbers.

Child abuse, sexual immorality, homosexuality, pornography, and demonically inspired movies, music, and other materials are common nowadays. Next time you go to the mall, notice the stores selling demonically oriented materials—everything from music, movies, and comic books to role-playing video games. You may be surprised to discover that many of these products package ancient cultic deities right along with their fictional characters, themes, and plot lines. Many cartoon shows directed at children do the same. While some of these forms of entertainment may be innocuous, others are not. Frequently exposure to these materials is the cause of demonic activity in an individual's life. Once these doors are opened, other demons take advantage of the opportunity to exert their negative influences.

CHRISTIANS ARE HURTING TOO

Besides the more obvious areas of demonic attack mentioned above, many sincere Christians are hurting because of the direct, oppressive activity of evil spirits. While scholars offer interesting theories and theologians debate concerning whether or not a Christian can be demon-possessed, demon-oppressed, or otherwise demonized, many people are facing bona fide demonic confrontations in their everyday lives. Multitudes of Christians admit to being in bondage to feelings, thoughts, and actions they know are incompatible with their faith. They feel strongly, irresistibly drawn toward evil, often compulsively repeating sins that repulse them, yet against which they feel powerless. Often this bondage can be traced to one of two areas: sexual immorality or rebellion against spiritual authority (especially parental authority). Frequently it involves both.

Beth, a petite blonde who had been "born and raised" in a Christian home, began dating when she was only thirteen years old. By the time she was fifteen, she had already had several sexual partners. She began drinking alcoholic beverages and doing drugs about the same time. By age sixteen she was tangled up in a strange relationship with a young man who abused her verbally, physically, and sexually. Yet she felt powerless to walk away from him. They'd break up on Saturday night, but by Monday afternoon he'd apologize and promise never to mistreat Beth again, and she would take him back.

Beth's parents were beside themselves. They had done their best to raise their daughter in what they felt was the right way.

They loved her dearly and had given her the best of everything they could afford. Beth's rebelliousness didn't make any sense to them. Why would she rebel so belligerently when her parents had been so good to her? They prayed for Beth constantly and enlisted others in their extended family and circle of friends to pray for Beth too, but she continued in her self-destructive patterns.

Her parents grounded her, not allowing her to see her friends, and especially her boyfriend, but she would sneak out of the house at night, often returning home just before daybreak, drunk or high on drugs, disheveled, and severely bruised. Her dad drove her to and from school every day in an attempt to keep her away from the negative influence of her so-called friends. Once, after Beth's dad had dropped her off in front of the school, Beth's boyfriend and several of his buddies surrounded the car and threatened to kill Beth's dad unless he stopped hassling his daughter.

Nothing anybody said or did could dissuade Beth from going back to her abusive boyfriend. Then one night, after guzzling more than a few beers with their friends, Beth's boyfriend "magnanimously" decided to pass her around to his buddies. Beth resisted, and in the struggle that followed, her boyfriend's buddies raped her and nearly killed her. When they were finished, they dumped Beth on her front lawn in the wee hours of the morning and drove off, roaring with laughter. That's where Beth's parents found her when the sun came up.

Beth's father was so furious that he took down a hunting rifle from his gun closet and started to go after the thugs who had raped his daughter. Only Beth's distraught cries of protest kept him from becoming a vigilante. Beth's mom wanted to call the police, but Beth refused to press charges. Finally, after an exam at the hospital, she agreed to see their pastor instead.

The family's minister, Pastor Reynolds, was a kind, grayhaired, grandfatherly man. He was aware of Beth's situation and had been praying for her for some time. Pastor Reynolds knew, however, that little lasting change would take place until Beth herself sought freedom from her bondage. Now that time had come.

The pastor felt strongly that because of Beth's sexual immorality and her use of drugs, she had opened the door to demonic involvement in her life, providing the enemy an easily accessed stronghold. Consequently Pastor Reynolds asked Beth and her parents if they would agree to have a team of Christian men and women assist them in dealing with the demons that were so powerfully influencing Beth's life. Beth and her parents didn't know much about demonic activity or what was involved in being delivered from it, but they trusted the pastor and agreed.

The group met in the church sanctuary on Sunday evening: Beth, her parents, Pastor Reynolds, Beth's youth pastor, two elders of the church, and several other men and women experienced in exorcisms. Pastor Reynolds only half-jokingly referred to the additional helpers as his "deliverance team."

Pastor Reynolds instructed Beth and the others that it was important that they begin by repenting of all known sin. Beth's parents asked God to forgive them for failing to be better parents. Beth asked God to forgive her for her sinful behavior and attitudes. Others in the group repented of sins as well.

Then Pastor Reynolds told the group he was going to speak directly to the demonic forces that were influencing Beth. "Get out of Beth's life," he said in a normal voice, but with great firmness. "She does not belong to you anymore. In the name of the Lord Jesus Christ, I command you to come out of her and leave her alone."

Sure enough, as soon as Pastor Reynolds began rebuking the demons, Beth's eyes and facial features began to change. Her eyes took on a faraway look, as though she were looking at something in the back of the church. Her face became gnarled, and

9

her lips began to quiver. Finally in a voice that sounded more like a man's than Beth's, she bellowed, "You can't have her. She's mine!"

Most of the people in the room instinctively stepped backward in shock. Pastor Reynolds, however, held his ground and looked directly into Beth's eyes as he spoke quietly but emphatically. "You are a liar. Jesus Christ is Lord. Jesus defeated Satan on the cross, and you are defeated along with him. Let go of this girl and come out of her."

Beth threw up all over Pastor Reynolds.

The pastor remained undaunted. He asked one of the women, who was praying along with the other members of the deliverance team, to go to the restroom and bring back some paper towels. When she returned, he casually wiped off the vomit and continued speaking to the demonic forces within Beth as though nothing unusual had happened.

Unlike the deliverance sessions portrayed in the movies or in novels, this session took some time. In fact, it went on for hours. The demonic influences seemed to come and go in Beth's personality. At times she was mean and loud, spewing filthy language at the pastor and her parents. At other times Beth was her normal self. The demons within her responded most violently when members of the group read Scripture to Beth.

During a period when Beth was calm, Pastor Reynolds asked her about the necklace and matching bracelet she was wearing. Both were made of gold and had a starlike charm attached. "Where did you get the pretty pendant?" the pastor asked.

"My boyfriend gave it to me," Beth replied honestly.

"And the bracelet too?" Pastor Reynolds inquired quietly.

"Yes, he gave me that too."

"I think it might be best if you took those off," Pastor Reynolds replied.

"What? Are you serious?" Beth asked incredulously.

"Yes. Would you mind? I don't understand it completely, but I know sometimes these pendants can be satanic symbols. They have no power in themselves, but the demons use them in the same way we do a flag, as a reminder of our allegiance. You're welcome to put them back on if there is nothing to be concerned about."

Beth reluctantly reached her arms toward the back of her neck to undo the clasp of the necklace, but as her hands got about shoulder high, she let out a scream. "I can't move my arms!" she shrieked.

Pastor Reynolds and the group moved closer to Beth and began praying for her in the name of Jesus, but they did not remove the necklace or bracelet from her. "I believe you must remove the necklace yourself, Beth," Pastor Reynolds to her. "We will pray for you and against the demons, but you must remove the jewelry yourself."

"I can't!" she wailed.

"Yes, you can," Pastor Reynolds said, "and you must."

For the next forty-five minutes Beth looked as though she were working out on an isometric unit at a gymnasium. As she raised her arms to remove the necklace, it was like an invisible "spotter" was pushing back against her. When she put her hands down, she could relax and rest, but as soon as she made a move toward the necklace or bracelet, she encountered resistance.

Near exhaustion and with tears streaming down her face, Beth shouted, "I don't want anything more to do with you, devil. I don't want your drugs. I don't want your sex. I don't want your booze. I don't want *you*!" And with that she reached her hands behind her neck, undid the clasp on the necklace, and threw it across the sanctuary. She did the same with the bracelet.

Almost immediately a beautiful calm came over Beth. She sat

down on the floor and began to cry softly, only these were tears of joy. Then she raised her hands and her face upward, and kept repeating quietly, "Thank You, Jesus. Thank You, Jesus!"

That was more than three years ago. Since then Beth has experienced a few setbacks as well as several encounters with demonic forces attempting to return to her life—the enemy does not give up territory easily. But Beth has stayed true to Jesus. Now when the demonic attacks come, she quickly calls upon her spiritual leaders to pray for her and with her. She is drug- and alcohol-free and has committed herself to waiting until marriage before she engages in sexual intercourse. "I feel like a virgin all over again," she said. "It's like God has forgiven me and wiped away my past. I'm clean, and I want to stay that way."

IT IS NO TIME TO BE NAÏVE

Understand, experiencing sexual temptation or an increased desire to be independent of authority is not necessarily sinful. But when you give in to improper sexual expressions or disrespectful attitudes toward authority, you offer the enemy a foothold in your life. Surprisingly many Christians recognize that something is amiss. They know that for some reason their Christian lives are not "working"; yet, like Beth, few suspect the possibility of a demonic dimension to their problems. Consequently the devil's forces continue to ride roughshod over many Christians. Unchallenged, the demonic influences do not go away; they expand their areas of operation, taking even more spiritual ground away from the person they are attacking.

In this book you will discover how you can discern the devil's devious devices. You will learn to recognize Satan for who he is, what his goals are, how he plans to attack you, and how you can arm and defend yourself and overcome the forces of hell. You'll find frank information to help you avoid opening the doors that might give the devil an opportunity to influence your life. You'll also explore ways of telling whether someone you love is under a demonic influence and what you can do about it. Most of all you will discover that Jesus has defeated the devil on the cross, and He can and will defeat him on a daily basis in your life if you will allow Him to do so.

I must warn you that some of what you are about to encounter may shock you. It might shake your status quo. Many contemporary Christians have been sleeping with the enemy for so long that they have grown accustomed to his influences. They are truly surprised to learn how the devil and his cohorts have been dangling them over hell, like puppets on a string, while the flames lick ever higher.

In some ways I hope this book will make you angry. Angry at sin. Angry at Satan. Angry at the way he has deceived so many of your friends and family members. I hope you will get mad enough to do something about it, mad enough to stand up and fight back in the power of Jesus's name.

You will not be alone. God is raising an army of men and women who are dedicated to Jesus Christ, operating in the power of the Holy Spirit and taking back the territory Satan has stolen. They are putting on the full armor of God, using the spiritual weapons and the authority God has given them, and are saying, "Satan, we're not going to take your guff anymore. You are a liar. You are not equal with God; you are nothing more than a created being, and Jesus Christ has defeated you. So take your filthy hands off us. We belong to Jesus, and you have no business messing with God's property."

As in any war not everyone will participate by fighting on the front lines. Indeed relatively few "foot soldiers" will wield their swords in hand-to-hand combat with the enemy, but all members of God's army need to know how and what to do if attacked.

When it comes to spiritual warfare, most of us will be involved behind the front lines. God needs "doctors" and "nurses" who can lovingly and compassionately treat wounded warriors. He assigns some as encouragers who will offer words of inspiration. He deploys people who will pray for those on the front lines and pray against the demonic forces of opposition.

God also will use people who fight through praise. Real spiritual power is released as God's people praise Him—something we all can do. The enemy hates to hear those praises, and although he puts up a fuss, Satan routinely retreats from any place where the name of Jesus is exalted.

However and wherever the Lord calls you to become involved in spiritual warfare, your main concern should be obedience to your "Commander's" voice. You don't need to know all the answers, or all the questions, for that matter. Your ready response simply needs to be, "Here am I, Lord; send me. I'm reporting for duty wherever You want me to go and whatever You want me to do." As you obey Him, the battles will be won, "'not by might nor by power, but by My Spirit,' says the LORD of hosts" (Zech. 4:6).

So come along. Let me give you some tips that will help you get ready to enter the war zone. But first, a word of caution...

Chapter Two

SNAKE IN THE GRASS

SOMETHING MUST BE wrong with my brain. I actually enjoy mowing the lawn. Honest. I know that may seem weird to you, especially if you regard cutting the grass as a truly tedious task. Maybe I spend so much time cooped up in an office that getting out in the air for an hour or two delights me, even if I must push a mower to do it.

One hot summer day years ago when we actually *pushed* our mowers manually, I was merrily mowing along when I felt something wrap around my ankle. I didn't pay much attention at first and pushed the mower a few steps forward. Thinking that my shoestring had come untied, I paused momentarily, while still mowing, and glanced down toward my shoe. There, to my surprise, instead of a loose shoestring I saw a blue-gray-colored snake wrapping itself around my leg.

Simultaneously I yelled *"Arrragghh!"* (or some similar, spiritual-sounding phrase), shoved the mower ahead a few feet, and jerked my leg away from the snake. Then in one continuous motion I swung around, grabbed the mower, which was still running, and pulled it back over top of the snake, cutting it to bits.

I stopped long enough to make sure the snake was dead (believe me, it was *dead*), then cranked up the motor on my mower and continued cutting the rest of the lawn. Only now my eyes were glued to the ground. "Where there's one snake, there are probably two or three more," I thought.

Funny, prior to encountering that blue-gray reptile, I rarely thought about snakes in our yard. I loved mowing the lawn every week, enjoyed being outdoors, and waved to the neighbors as they drove by; I was totally oblivious to the existence of any blue-gray snakes. Now, however, I saw "snakes" everywhere: in the bushes, under rocks, in the weeds. I was certain our yard was infested with serpents. Sticks and twigs that had fallen from the trees looked like snakes to me. Leaves blowing across the lawn, brushing against my ankles caused me to whirl around in alarm.

A sweet little lady I met at the post office told me that snakes didn't like mothballs. That was good enough for me. I went out and bought a case of mothballs and lined the perimeter of our property with them. I'm not sure what effect the smell of the mothballs had on the local snake population, but I didn't see a moth for months! And no friends or neighbors came to visit.

TWO EXTREMES TO AVOID

Many Christians respond similarly to spiritual warfare, leaning toward either an underemphasis or an overemphasis on the subject. Some Christians merrily mow their way through life, oblivious to the existence of the supernatural battle that is raging all around them or to their own immediate danger of being attacked. Meanwhile the serpent wraps himself around their legs, ready to sink his fangs into their flesh whenever he desires to do so.

Understandably many people have been "spooked" by all the talk about demons in recent years. In most every town you can find a group of people regarded as "crazies" by the local population because they are attempting to cast the demons out of everything from dance halls to mud flaps. Not wanting to be associated with "that" crowd, many Christians make the mistake of ignoring spiritual warfare altogether. Their idea that "If we don't talk about the devil, maybe he'll go away!" is as ludicrous as saying, "If we don't talk about nuclear war, racism, political oppression, or impending ecological disasters, all that scary stuff will disappear." No, it won't. When it comes to spiritual warfare, ignorance is not bliss.

Satan will not slip back under a rock somewhere if you ignore him. You have to shake him off your leg, get him off your case. The devil doesn't go away because you don't believe in him. He won't leave you alone simply because you leave him alone.

On the other hand some Christians are like I was after seeing the snake. Although I saw only one snake in one part of the yard, I suddenly started seeing "snakes" everywhere. Similarly some Christians genuinely experience a bona fide supernatural encounter with the devil or, more likely, some of his demons. But then they start attributing to demons everything or anything semi-bad that happens in their lives. In doing so, they are abdicating their own responsibility for their actions and attitudes, which is the exact opposite of what the Scriptures teach.

Maybe you've met some people who tend to blame everything negative in their lives on demonic activity. They have a demon of overeating or a demon of cigarette smoking or demons of lust or gambling. If they fail to get a promotion at work, a demon was interfering with their ability to think clearly (while they conveniently ignore the fact that they did not adequately prepare for the interview and have been doing shoddy work in the position they currently hold). If the car won't start, there's a demon in the engine. I've heard demons blamed for everything from tooth decay to bounced checks to laziness, to an inability to get a date for the big event.

Rather than causing people to believe in the Lord (or the devil), such trivializing of demonic influences actually turns most people off from taking either seriously. By attributing everything to a demon, they play right into the enemy's hands by creating an aura of silliness around satanic activity.

Moreover many Christians who become preoccupied with demons don't seem to get along well with their fellow believers. Their lives are in constant conflict with something or somebody. The peace of God is rarely evident in them. Instead they are on edge, often judgmental and critical of their brothers and sisters, always looking for a fight. Everyone they know, it seems, has a demon of some kind.

John Dawson is a Bible teacher and author whose spiritual insights I greatly respect. Writing in the foreword to C. Peter Wagner's book *Engaging the Enemy*, John encourages caution and balance in our attitudes toward spiritual warfare:

> There has always been a danger of either denial of satanic activity altogether, or of focusing on it too much. If we gain knowledge of the name and nature of an evil spirit and publish it broadly, the enemy will only attempt to glorify himself openly or to instill fear among the immature. Joshua warned the Israelites about this temptation, "You shall not make mention of the name of their gods" (Joshua 23:7). Morbid fascination is a carnal appetite that can drive us to search out the hidden knowledge of the evil realm. The Bible says in Romans 16:19, "I want you to be wise in what is good, and innocent in what is evil." True, God reveals hidden mysteries to His close friends. "The secret of the Lord is with those who fear Him" (Psalm 25:14). However, the privilege of knowing God Himself should be the center of our desire.[1]

THE DEVIL DID NOT MAKE YOU DO IT!

The truth is, most of what you and I will deal with in our daily lives is *not* demonically inspired. It can be attributed to our own foolishness, faults, foibles, physical infirmities, quirks, peccadilloes, and idiosyncrasies. Furthermore we all carry around some banged-up emotional baggage from our childhoods. Lying beneath all this is the fact that we have been born into a sinful world and have an intrinsically sinful nature. For example, our parents never had to teach us to be selfish; looking out for number one came all too naturally.

With our innate inclination to please ourselves, it is easy to succumb to temptations of pleasure, greed, pride, lust, or anything else that caters to our self-interest. Not even the slightest satanic provocation or nudge is necessary to talk us into indulging our flesh. We are more than eager to do that on our own.

Any one of these factors can become a tool the devil uses against us. It's as though a thief were walking by your house one day and saw all the doors and windows flung wide open, with your most valuable possessions displayed unprotected, available for all to see. Nobody would be surprised if the thief came in and helped himself to your property.

Similarly when the enemy of your soul passes by and sees you unprotected, distracted from what really matters, spending most of your dwindling spiritual reserves struggling with habitual sins or speaking evil of someone else, he chortles, "All right! This is my kind of place. These are my kind of people. I think I should stay for a while. Better still, I think I'll just move in and make myself at home."

On the other hand, if your life is filled with the Holy Spirit, the Spirit of Jesus, when the devil comes knocking, Jesus answers the door. Satan instantly recognizes Jesus and knows he is powerless to touch what is His, so he quickly retreats. "Oops! Sorry. Wrong address. Actually, wrong neighborhood! In fact, I may be in the wrong town! 'Bye." Certainly this is an oversimplification, but it is an accurate portrayal of what happens when the devil comes calling on a Spirit-filled believer.

Our Lord Jesus is far greater and more powerful than Satan

and all his heinous hordes of hell combined. If your life is humbly submitted to the lordship of Christ and you confess your sins as the Holy Spirit convicts you, keeping "short accounts" with God, you have nothing to fear from the enemy. If you are trusting in Jesus, "God's Spirit is in you and is more powerful than the one that is in the world" (1 John 4:4, CEV). That means you have about as much chance of being possessed by a demon today as you do of being attacked by King Kong in the mall parking lot!

BALANCE IS THE KEY

Understand, I'm not trying to lull you into overconfidence or complacency. On the contrary, the whole purpose of this book is to help you become more aware of, and prepared for, the supernatural conflict that is going on all around you. Our focus, however, must always be on Jesus, not the devil. Satan relishes attention, and when we give him too much time or credit, the devil gets the glory rather than God. When that happens, the enemy wins a battle by default; he has succeeded in drawing our focus away from Christ without having to do a thing.

Avoid this mess. While you definitely do not want to be ignorant of the devil's devices, you need to concentrate on God's priorities for your life. His top two priorities for you are the same as those He has for the entire world: (1) He wants to save those who are lost and dying without a relationship with Jesus Christ; (2) He wants to help His family "grow up" spiritually and get ready to spend eternity with Him.

Of course these are precisely the priorities that Satan is hoping to block. Consequently as you become more concerned about and involved in the priorities that are upon God's heart, it makes sense that you will encounter opposition from Satan. Furthermore you are bound to bump into people who are living in bondage and need deliverance. As you do, you can be sure that the forces of hell will attempt to place obstacles in your path as you seek to set free those individuals Satan has been holding hostage.

But to be effective in spiritual warfare, as author Dean Sherman points out, you need to be *"aware of the enemy but impressed with God. It should never be the other way around. We should not be impressed with Satan and only aware of God. If we aren't careful, our conversations can focus on the amazing powers of darkness, and what all the devil is doing.... While we should never be awestruck by the enemy's activities, we must learn to see what he is trying to do in our lives. We must be able to say, 'This is a move of the enemy,' or, 'The devil is behind this.'"[2]*

IS IT SATAN OR PIZZA?

Many Christians have difficulty discerning whether their spiritual impressions are from God, Satan, circumstances, or a bad case of indigestion from eating too much pizza the previous night. How can you tell the difference?

First, Jesus said we would know His voice. In comparing Himself to a good shepherd, Christ said, "The sheep hear his voice, and he calls his own sheep by name and leads them out.... The sheep follow him because they know his voice. A stranger they simply will not follow, but will flee from him, because they do not know the voice of strangers" (John 10:3–5).

Then just in case anybody missed His point, Jesus said it even more specifically: "I am the good shepherd, and I know My own, and My own know Me.... My sheep hear My voice, and I know them, and they follow Me" (John 10:14, 27). Jesus was making it clear that if we know Him and are living in a close relationship with Him, we will have no trouble recognizing His voice.

My dad passed away in 1997, but for most of my life, whenever I called him on the telephone, I didn't need to say, "This is your middle son; remember me?" No, he recognized my voice instantly. When my dad called me, he never began the conversation by introducing himself. Usually the moment I picked up the phone, I'd hear his voice booming through the earpiece, "Hey, how ya doin'?" I never once asked, "Who is this?" I immediately recognized his voice.

Similarly when you are living in close relationship with Jesus, you know His voice, and equally important, especially in regard to spiritual warfare, you know when it is *not* His voice.

Second, some people have a valid spiritual gift of discerning or "distinguishing of spirits," as mentioned in 1 Corinthians 12:10. This is more than mere intuition or guesswork. It is a special ability the Holy Spirit gives to certain individuals. Like all spiritual gifts, it is meant to build up the body of Christ. When it is used correctly, this gift is frequently a means of great blessing to the kingdom, since the person who has the gift is able to supernaturally perceive the influence under which spirits are operating. Then that person, or others working together in a deliverance ministry, can often address the evil spirits by name and cast them out of a demonized person.

If the gift is misused, it can be a sideshow, an insult, or an extremely destructive mistake. After all, how would you feel if someone were claiming to recognize demons in you if there were none?

That's probably why the Holy Spirit does not give the gift of discerning of spirits to all of us. He knows we'd spend so much time looking for demons in one another we'd never get anything done for the kingdom of God. We'd also become so enamored with trying to discern counterfeit spirits, we might miss the real demonic spirits when they came along.

A GIFT IN THE NICK OF TIME

Although not all of us have the gift of discerning spirits, God often gives us the spiritual insight and wisdom we need to deal with an immediate situation. Early in my walk with the Lord I played drums for a contemporary Christian rock band made up of my family members and some friends. One night we were to do an evangelistic concert in an old theater building that had been used previously to show pornographic movies. The theater was dark and dingy and would have been a creepy place to play even if there were no evil spirits present. But there were.

As we unloaded our sound equipment and instruments and began setting up for the concert, the members of the band, one by one, started getting sick. We all felt a smothering sort of presence in the building, making it almost difficult to breathe. Still, we were relatively new Christians with limited experience in spiritual warfare, so we naively continued working despite the obvious presence in the building.

I went upstairs into the projection room to see if I could find some extra spotlights for the stage, but the projection room was bare except for some old take-up reels strewn around the floor. I closed the door, turned around, and started to descend the steep, narrow staircase leading down from the projection room. But just as I did, a powerful force—that is the only way I know to describe it—smacked right into me, literally throwing me backward, "spread eagle," onto the steps. I slid down several steps on my back before I realized what was happening. Dazed and instantly sick to my stomach, I slowly wobbled to my feet and made my way back downstairs into the theater.

I gathered our group together and said, "Gang, we need to pray. There's something weird about this place." I didn't need to convince the other members of the band. We stood in the theater and began praying. We prayed for our own protection. We prayed for the concert that night and for the people who would be coming. Then, although none of us were experts in spiritual warfare, the Lord gave several members of the group discernment that we should pray against the evil presence in the theater. So we did. It wasn't a fancy prayer or anything that might be considered profound. We were simply a group of young believers praying in Jesus's name and taking authority over the evil presence that lurked in that place. While we prayed, we all felt the presence lift from the theater.

That night we had a marvelous concert, and at the close of the service the entire front of the theater was lined six to ten people deep as young men and women repented of their sins, trusted Jesus as their Savior, and invited Him to take full control of their lives. My brother, John, was still preaching to the people when suddenly a young woman among the seekers began speaking out in tongues. Actually what she did sounded more like "shrieking in tongues." None of us would have been alarmed if the woman had been praising the Lord in an unknown tongue, but it was obvious that this woman was not exalting Jesus.

I was standing behind the drums, listening to my brother while intently praying for the people in the audience, but as soon as I heard the young woman's voice, I knew her outburst was not of God. I bounded out from behind the drums, grabbed a microphone, and spoke as firmly as I could, "In the name of Jesus, keep quiet! Our God is a God of order, and right now you are out of order." The woman fell instantly quiet, and the Lord swept through the theater with another powerful move of His Holy Spirit. Dozens of people poured to the front of the room to find Jesus.

Although I do not have an ongoing gift of discerning of spirits, occasionally the Lord has done something similar to what He did in the theater that night. He has given me an instantaneous, unusual ability to recognize something in the spirit realm that was either right or wrong. When the situation was addressed, the gift was gone. I couldn't look at the next situation and expect that same supernatural spiritual perception. What I could do, however, is the same thing you can do when you are not certain if something is "of the Lord" or is the work of the devil.

WHEN IN DOUBT, ASK!

Remember the theme song from the popular movie *Ghostbusters*, which was ostensibly a comedy about paranormal activity? If you have to call somebody, you don't want to call those guys!

When you need to know whether or not you are confronting a demonic situation, just *ask God*. He will be glad to let you know when the devil is at work in your midst. You don't have to stumble around in the dark, wondering whether you should rebuke something, embrace it, or ignore it. Ask the Lord to let you know what is going on in the circumstances you are facing and to show you how you should respond. Then do whatever He tells you to do to defeat the enemy.

It helps, though, if you know *who* and *why* we are fighting.

Chapter Three

WHERE DID SATAN COME FROM?

I WAS SITTING ONBOARD an airplane, flying back home to Nashville after a difficult week of evangelistic meetings in Pennsylvania, where I had been speaking. We had won many outstanding spiritual victories that week, but the enemy had given us fits. One of the leaders of the church summed up the week when he said, "Satan has had a stranglehold on this church and town for years. Now, finally, it has been broken." I knew he was right, but I also knew we had been in a close fight with the devil all week long.

I was bone tired—emotionally and physically depleted as I slumped down farther in my seat and began reading a book. A young man sitting next to me noticed the title of my book and asked, "Are you a Christian?"

"Yes, I am," I replied groggily.

"Well, great, brother; I'm glad to meet you!" he gushed. He told me his name and that he was a student at a well-respected Christian university. Although I was happy to meet another Christian on the plane, I really wasn't in much of a mood for talking to the young man. It didn't matter. He talked enough for both of us.

I listened idly to his stories, trying my best to remain interested. He told me about his family, his girlfriend, and his ministry plans. I nodded politely in all the right places. I was genuinely happy for the guy, but I was just too tired to offer much in the way of exciting conversation.

The young man aroused my interest, though, when he began talking about the spiritual warfare taking place on his campus. "Satan is really working overtime at our college," he told me. "Why just today we had a situation where we had to cast the devil out of a student. Satan has been after our college all year."

"Hmm, that's interesting," I thought. I just left one part of Pennsylvania where the congregation was fighting Satan. Now here is this guy telling me that Satan is alive and well and wreaking havoc on his college campus, all the way across the state. "That Satan must be a fast traveler," I mused.

When I arrived home later that night, I turned on a television program on which the hosts of a Christian talk show were discussing what Satan was doing just then in their city—nearly fifteen hundred miles away from Pennsylvania. "Unbelievable!"I thought. "The devil seems to be everywhere."

The great preacher Billy Sunday used to ask his congregations, "How many of you have personally met the devil today?" If only a smattering of people raised their hands, Sunday would quip, "Well, if you haven't met the devil today face-to-face, you're probably going the same direction he is!"[1] Most members of the audience would laugh, but many took Sunday's words literally.

Have you ever wondered how Satan can be in so many places at one time? The truth is: he can't. Satan is a created being; therefore, he can only be in one place at a time. The devil is not omnipresent like God, who can be everywhere at once.

How, then, can the devil be in thousands of places at one time, planting evil suggestions in people's minds and tempting them to disobey God? Satan does so by dispatching demonic forces, fallen angels, to various locations around the world.

Nobody on earth knows how many demons the devil has at his disposal, but we do know the number is limited. Satan cannot create anything, so he doesn't have the power to spawn more demons. He must stick with those he has.

A War in Heaven

The big question is: Where did these evil, supernatural beings come from? Obviously God did not create them to be the devil and his demons. Everything God made was good (Gen. 1:31). But something went wrong. Somehow, somewhere, apparently prior to the creation of man, a rebellion took place in heaven. A mighty angelic creature known as Lucifer—the name comes from the Latin translation of "morning star" (Isa. 14:12, NIV)—led a vast army of angels in opposition to the Lord God. The Bible records few details of this rebellion, but a strong hint suggests that Lucifer was the angel that later became known as Satan.

Although he is not named specifically, many Bible scholars believe Lucifer is implicated in Ezekiel 28:12, 14: "You had the seal of perfection, full of wisdom and perfect in beauty.... You were the anointed cherub who covers, and I placed you there. You were on the holy mountain of God."

The prophetic passage seems to have a triple fulfillment, one each in the future, present, and past. The future reference is to the "beast," revealed in Revelation 13:4, also known as the Antichrist, who is under the direct control of Satan. The contemporary fulfillment of the prophecy in Ezekiel's day pointed to the king of Babylon, the despot who had plundered Jerusalem and hauled God's people into exile. The ancient past fulfillment is thought to be a reference to Lucifer.

Lucifer must have been quite a good-looking creature, since his beautiful appearance is mentioned in the Bible, while that of most other angels is not. Like Gabriel and Michael, Lucifer was privileged to stand before God, worshipping Him and awaiting His instructions. Lucifer was also extremely wise (Ezek. 28:12).

Apparently Lucifer was highly involved in heaven's music program, as Scripture calls attention to the workmanship of the settings and sockets of Lucifer's tambourines and flutes (Ezek. 28:13). Well-known worship leader LaMar Boschman believes this biblical text implies that Lucifer led worship in heaven.[2] If so, perhaps that partly explains Satan's interest in music. More than any other fallen angel he knows the power that music can have in a person's life, either positively or negatively.

Other scholars believe Lucifer was more of a super-guard, sort of a heavenly secret service agent, as suggested by the phrase "the cherub who covers" (Ezek. 28:14). God Himself gave Lucifer this special authority. Regardless of his exact role Lucifer had direct access to God and held an office or position unequaled in the angelic realm.

We don't know how long the Lord tolerated Lucifer's rebellion, but we do know that one day Lucifer was cast out of the presence of God and out of heaven. Why did all this happen? What did Lucifer do that was so wrong? A further and more puzzling question is how sin could exist in heaven, a kingdom of complete sinlessness. More specifically how could sinless angels sin against God?

Scripture doesn't say. The Bible simply sets forth the record as fact, similar to the unexplained, "In the beginning God" (Gen. 1:1). No attempt is made to explain God's existence; it is simply declared. Similarly Lucifer's fall and subsequent renaming as Satan are considered a given by most biblical writers.

In the same way that our heavenly Father created us as more than mere automatons, human robots He could maneuver at will for His pleasure, God also gave some sort of free will to His angels. Even Lucifer and the other angels had to choose to obey or disobey Him.

The details of how Lucifer was transformed from a shining, high-ranking angel into the liar, thief, and murderer he has become are not told in the Bible. Any stories you might read or hear describing that event are based on conjecture or someone's overactive imagination. Obviously God did not intend for us to dwell upon the devil's demise, or He would have provided more information.

We do know, however, that Satan deceived a large number of God's angels into following him, and like their master, these angels were cast out of heaven. Scripture says that the great red dragon's tail "swept away a third of the stars of heaven and threw them to the earth" (Rev. 12:4). Many Bible scholars believe these "falling stars" are a reference to the devil's depopulation of heaven. In Revelation 12:9 the dragon is explained to be "the serpent of old who is called the devil and Satan, who deceives the whole world."

Nowhere in Scripture is there even the slightest hint that Satan and his demons will ever be saved, reformed, and allowed to reenter the kingdom of God. On the contrary, the Bible is replete with references to Satan's eventual destruction, as well as that of anyone who follows him. The apostle John recorded the final word on the devil and his fiendish followers:

> And I saw the beast and the kings of the earth and their armies, assembled to make war against Him who sat upon the horse, and against His army.
>
> And the beast was seized, and with him the false prophet who performed the signs in his presence, by which he deceived those who had received the mark of the beast and those who worshiped his image; these two were thrown alive into the lake of fire which burns with brimstone....And the devil who deceived them was thrown into the lake of fire and brimstone, where the beast and the false prophet are also; and they will be tormented day and night forever and ever.
>
> —REVELATION 19:19–20; 20:10

The devil and his demons know they are doomed. They hate God and will never repent, even though they tremble at their imminent, eternal torment in the lake of fire.

IT's a Matter of Choice

Lucifer was cast out of heaven because of his own choices. He said, "I will ascend to heaven; I will raise my throne above the stars of God, and I will sit on the mount of assembly in the recesses of the north. I will ascend above the heights of the clouds; I will make myself like the Most High" (Isa. 14:13–14). Lucifer was declaring that he would be another god just like the one true God. That was his desire when he rebelled against God, and to this day he has not deviated from that plan.

But God was not about to sit by and watch while Lucifer rebelled. God has always punished rebellion against Him, and He always will. The Scripture continues: "Nevertheless you will be thrust down to Sheol, to the recesses of the pit. Those who see you will gaze at you, they will ponder over you, saying, 'Is this the man who made the earth tremble, who shook kingdoms, who made the world like a wilderness and overthrew its cities, who did not allow his prisoners to go home?'" (Isa. 14:15–17).

One day soon this prophecy will be completely fulfilled. People who formerly feared Satan and his heinous assistants will look at them and say, "Is that all there was to them?" Many Christians are adopting this attitude now.

Steve has taken two short-term mission trips. As part of his pretrip training he learned basic principles of spiritual warfare, which increased his faith and provided him tremendous confidence in his spiritual life.

"There was a time," Steve explained, "when I was scared stiff of anything that had to do with the devil or demons. Then I learned who they are—merely fallen angels, created beings— and that even as a relatively new Christian, with Jesus in the driver's seat of my life, I have more supernatural power available to me than all the demons of hell. Now when the devil or one of his demons tries to bother me, I simply say, "Oh, it's you. In the name of Jesus, get out of here!"

Steve has the right idea. While we never want to underestimate the enemy, many people, Christians included, think Lucifer is like another god. They believe God is the God of good and Satan is the god of evil; God and Satan are seen as equals, standing in opposition. The devil has duped millions into believing this lie.

Understand: God and Satan are not equal counterparts. Only God is God. He is the Creator. He is eternal and infinite. He is omniscient (all-knowing), omnipotent (all-powerful), omnipresent (everywhere at all times), and sovereign (having supreme authority).

Lucifer is simply a fallen archangel—created, finite, and limited in knowledge and ability. He doesn't know everything. He can't do everything. He can't read your mind. Furthermore, as mentioned previously, he can be in only one place at one time.

Jesus referred to Satan as "the ruler of this world" (John 12:31), and the apostle Paul further indicted the devil by saying, "The god of this world has blinded the minds of the unbelieving so that they might not see the light of the gospel of the glory of Christ, who is the image of God" (2 Cor. 4:4).

Still it would be wrong to assume that Satan has absolute power on the earth. The story of Job in the Old Testament shows us otherwise. Satan could not touch Job without God's permission, and even then he could not kill him. Satan engineered a series of disasters intended to make "righteous and upright" Job curse God. But despite one satanically inspired tragedy after another, Job continued to trust God, and the devil was defeated in his life.

How is Satan the ruler of this world then? He is ruler of

the world's systems of thought and values. Paul's words in 2 Corinthians 4:4 could be read "god of this age," implying, as Paul explains, that Satan causes people to believe lies that blind them to the truth about Jesus. In other words, Satan's "kingdom" is built upon deception; he is the ruler of a house of cards, and one day soon it is all going to crumble.

HOW COULD SATAN BE SO STUPID?

It was ridiculous for Satan to attempt to usurp God's authority. In a million years Satan could never be like God. It is simply not possible for the created being to become his own Creator. God is God, and nothing in the universe can compare to Him. Certainly human beings were made in His image, but people at their best are neither all-knowing, all-powerful, nor able to be in more than one place at a time. When Scripture says we are made in God's image, it is His moral image that we are meant to reflect, not His physical characteristics.

If it was so impossible for Lucifer to become like God, why did he try? The answer can be found within each of us. Every one of us has tried something similar; we have attempted to be the master of our own universe, the captain of our own ship, the boss, the head honcho, the number-one man or woman. Whatever you want to call it, when we determine in our hearts to live without God, when we say, "I don't need anyone else to run my life," what we are really saying is, "I can be my own god. I am the most important being in my universe."

What Lucifer the powerful archangel did was absolutely ludicrous. Yet we, as weak, finite beings, subject to everything from cancer to dementia to acne, think we can run our own lives without God. What a joke! What arrogance. To try to live without God is to try to be God. Absurd, insane pride entered Satan's heart and, sadly, we have all been exposed to this; it is an extremely contagious disease.

WHAT'S IN A NAME?

In recent years the name of Satan has been used frequently in derision. Comedians such as Flip Wilson ("The devil made me do it!"[3]) and *Saturday Night Live's* infamous "Church Lady," Dana Carvey ("Could it be…Saaa—tan?"[4]) have trivialized the devil's name. Islamic terrorists have branded the United States and Israel as "the Great Satan" and "the Little Satan." No doubt the devil doesn't mind. After all, if he can keep you laughing and making light of his existence, or confused regarding his role in international affairs, you will be poorly prepared to defend yourself against any demonic onslaughts he may launch.

However, contrary to the frivolous image of Satan presented by comedians or the misguided attributions of anti-Christian, anti-Jewish governmental leaders, Satan is evil, and his name itself has become a symbol of evil. *Satan* literally means "adversary," or, "one who stands against or in opposition to."[5] That's who he is. He is your archenemy, standing in opposition to all the things God wants to do in and through your life.

At times the word *Satan* is used in the Bible to refer to his demonic forces, not simply to the individual, Lucifer. (In this book I will do the same; I will use the name Satan to refer to the devil himself or his host of demonic fallen angels.) Nevertheless it is vital to understand that the being called Satan is merely a fallen angel. He is our adversary, and we must consider him to be that, no more and no less.

When Lucifer was cast out of heaven, he took many of the angels with him. The Bible does not clearly say so, but it seems reasonable that these fallen angels are now what the Bible calls demons, evil spirits, or unclean spirits. These spirits are real personalities. We are not fighting "the force" or some mystical, impersonal evil power or all-pervading energy. Jesus didn't confront a nebulous force of evil. Christ confronted evil spirits, and He cast them out of the person they inhabited.

Like all personalities, fallen angels can think, listen, communicate, experience, act, and react. From the biblical record concerning angels and demons, we know they are able to interact with humans. Apparently they have the ability to speak to us in our minds. (For instance, the devil put it into Judas's mind to betray Christ, according to John 13:2.) They hear what we say, watch our reactions, and plan their strategies of attack at our areas of weakness.

Because these evil personalities listen, we need to speak to them when we enter into spiritual warfare. Some Christians may be reluctant to address the enemy. The Bible is clear, however, that we are to resist the powers of darkness (James 4:7; 1 Pet. 5:9). How do we resist a personality? Should we wave our Bibles, put up billboards, wear our witness T-shirts, close our eyes, or hold our breath? The only way I know to resist a personality, short of a fistfight, is to speak words of resistance.

The brilliant, self-taught minister A. W. Tozer preached often a sermon titled "I Talk Back to the Devil." Tozer had the right idea. Christians are to address Satan and the powers of darkness directly, rebuking them and verbally denying them access to our lives. Jesus addressed the enemy directly. Having told us that we would do greater things than He (John 14:12), Jesus has shown us by example that we too should address the enemy, resisting him and taking authority over him.

In Mark 16:17 Jesus commissioned us to use His name in coming against the enemy. He didn't say He would confront the devil and his demons for us—He said that in His name *we* would cast out devils.

But before we delve into that subject, we'd better look more closely at how we got involved in this fight in the first place. You may recall it began in a garden.

Chapter Four

HOW DID WE GET INVOLVED?

S PIRITUAL WARFARE AS we know it today began in the Garden of Eden. God created Adam and Eve and placed them in an idyllic paradise. Imagine how incredible that must have been!

Consider this: You wake up one morning on a fabulous tropical island; you roll over on the ground where you have been sleeping and notice for the first time that you have been sleeping in your "birthday suit." And what a birthday suit it is. Your body is perfect in every way: perfect skin; perfect hair; perfect muscles; perfectly straight, white teeth; and a smile that could knock 'em dead from across the room.

Then you hear a rustling behind you, and you quickly turn around to see…oh, my! Hold onto your heart. Standing right there before you is the most gorgeous creature you have ever seen! Perfect body; perfect hair; perfect teeth…why, it looks as though the two of you were made for each other!

You are both naked, yet you sense no shame or embarrassment because God brought you two together. It was the first marriage ceremony every performed. No bridesmaids or groomsmen were in attendance, but you had the feeling that all of history was looking over your shoulder. And those vows. You'll never forget those words:

This is now bone of my bones, and flesh of my flesh; she shall be called Woman, because she was taken out of Man.

—GENESIS 2:23

Then God Himself pronounced you husband and wife by saying, "For this reason a man shall leave his father and his mother, and be joined to his wife; and they shall become one flesh" (Gen. 2:24).

What a life! Just the two of you, living in love with each other and in harmony with nature. Who could ask for anything more? Yet there is more. God Himself walks with you and talks with you. You don't have a bunch of rules and regulations in order to get to know Him; you have a special relationship with Him, an intimate communion with God in which you can enjoy His presence all the time.

Every day is another day in paradise. You actually enjoy doing the work of cultivating the garden. It's all there for your pleasure. You can do anything you want; you can eat from every plant in the place…except that one tree in the middle of the garden from which God forbids you to eat. *Hmm, that one tree. I wonder what is so special about that forbidden fruit…*

Adam and Eve had it made until Satan launched his first attack upon humanity. The pattern of Satan's deceit and the actions and reactions of Adam and Eve have been repeated in spiritual warfare down through history. Let's take a look.

THE ROAD TO DESTRUCTION

Eve was out walking around all by herself one day when the devil approached her with the subtly worded question: "Indeed, has God said, 'You shall not eat from any tree of the garden'?" (Gen. 3:1). Right then and there Eve should have shut the devil down and told him to keep quiet. But she didn't. She entertained his question and entered into a discussion with the devil, a conversation manipulated and controlled by Satan. Although she didn't know it at the time (as far as we know, she had never seen or heard from the devil before this), Eve violated the first of five basic rules of spiritual warfare, which we will discuss in the next two chapters:

1. Never, ever enter into a dialogue with the devil on his terms.

If you are being tempted or taunted by the devil or one of his demons, do what Jesus did. He answered Satan's snide remarks by saying, "Away from me, Satan! For it is written..." (Matt. 4:10; NIV). Jesus wasn't taking any lip from the devil. Instead He used the "sword of the Spirit, which is the word of God" (Eph. 6:17), and answered the devil directly from the Scriptures. You can do the same.

Eve did not enjoy the luxury of having the *written* Word of God at her disposal. Obviously the Bible hadn't been written yet. Still, she had God's personal word to her and Adam. She knew what God had said. God had not forbidden Adam and Eve to eat from *any* tree of the garden, as the devil had said. Quite the contrary, they *could* eat from any tree... except one, the tree of the knowledge of good and evil. But the devil twisted God's words and deceived Eve, causing her to violate another basic rule of spiritual warfare:

2. Never, ever entertain devilish thoughts about God's goodness.

Maybe as Eve considered Satan's suggestion, she said to herself, "Yes, that's right! I mean, after all, why did God put that forbidden fruit in front of my face anyhow, right where I have to see it every day? It's just not fair. It's almost as if God wants me to fail." We all have doubts from time to time. Often your doubts can lead to stronger faith in Jesus Christ, especially when you are grappling with issues of how your faith and reason fit together. Doubt does not necessarily imply unbelief or a lack of faith. Author Winkie Pratney offers this wise distinction between doubt and unbelief:

> Unbelief is "I don't care what God says; I'm not going to do it." Unbelief is the refusal to commit yourself to something seen quite clearly as true....Doubt is "I am in two minds about it. I don't know what to do. I'm up in the air about it. I'm hesitating. I'm not sure..." Doubt is not the opposite of faith. When you doubt, it is not some cowardly betrayal of Jesus and a surrender to the wrong side. The relationship between doubt and faith is more like the relationship between courage and fear. The opposite of courage is cowardice, not fear. Here's a person in a war who, though he is afraid, lets courage master his fear and goes ahead and does it anyway....So faith doesn't mean that you will have no doubt. It just means that one overrules the other.[1]

When Satan twisted God's Word about which fruits she and Adam could eat, he was subtly raising doubt in Eve's mind about the Lord's goodness toward them. It was as if the devil were saying, "See how mean God is! He is denying you all the delicacies in this garden. How can God possibly be good and treat you like this? He doesn't love you; He doesn't have your best interests at heart. He just wants to keep you from enjoying life." All this and more was wrapped up in the devil's deceptive question to Eve.

What a liar! No wonder Jesus said the devil "was a murderer from the beginning, and does not stand in the truth because there is no truth in him. Whenever he speaks a lie, he speaks from his own nature, for he is a liar and the father of lies" (John 8:44).

The enemy's tactics haven't changed much over the years.

Satan whispers those surly doubts in our mind: "See, God isn't really good. How could God be good and allow you to go through so many tough times? How could God be good when He denies you what you want more than anything else in the world? How could God be good and allow your spouse to file for divorce, or the person you loved and trusted most to walk out of your life? How could God be good and yet do nothing to prevent child abuse, world hunger, or cancer?"

We've all heard those questions in our minds. To question why bad things happen to good people or to doubt is not sin, but when we allow those questions to turn into unbelief, it is an insult to God. Moreover, any time you entertain a doubt that casts a reproach upon God's goodness, you are heading in the wrong direction and opening the door to demonic deception. God's goodness is part of His character, which is revealed throughout the Bible. To question His goodness is to doubt everything about His will for your life.

Eve took a second step toward destruction when she allowed that sort of devilish doubt to continue. She didn't invite the devil's doubts, but as soon as she recognized Satan's insult to God, she should have told the devil to take a hike.

Understand, the enemy will assault your mind with doubts for as long as you allow him to do so. He attempts to undermine your faith in the Lord and your confidence in God's goodness by pointing out perceived inconsistencies in God's Word and God's actions. You need to recognize that for what it is, not merely an academic, intellectual question but a demonic attack.

Shannon, a first-year student at a large university, had committed her life to Christ as a child. She maintained her Christian faith and testimony throughout high school, despite the mockery of her friends and strong temptations to compromise. She entered college with both her values and her virginity intact.

During her first semester on the university campus Shannon

found her faith coming under constant fire. In her English literature courses as well as her science courses she felt as though the carpet were being pulled out from under her Christian faith. It seemed as though there was a concerted effort on the part of the university faculty to destroy her trust in Christ.

"I could have been an atheist, a radical feminist, a communist, or a Zen Buddhist, and everyone would have considered me a seeker of truth," Shannon said. "But because I announced that I was a Christian, I was regarded as an intellectual midget by my professors and my classmates. At first I tried to defend Christianity in class whenever one of my professors began a slanted tirade against Jesus, God, the church, or Christianity in general. But my profs skewered me. They had their material well prepared in advance and knew exactly how to trap me; they shredded my answers to their questions as easily as ice in a blender. Before long all my pat answers about the Bible began to melt away. Soon I stopped raising my hand in opposition to their acid comments about Christianity.

"I began to doubt God's existence. Maybe this Jesus stuff was something like belief in Santa Claus, a nice delusion when you're a kid, but not really something any educated person believes in real life. I heard all those questions so many times: 'If there is a good God, why does He allow suffering in the world; why does He allow little babies to die?' I began to think, 'Maybe they are right; maybe God, if He's there, can't or won't do anything to help me.' After a while my doubts began to get to me, and I started to come up with all the wrong answers.

"As I allowed those doubts to undermine my values, it wasn't long before my virginity seemed a rather silly thing to defend as well. I started hitting the party scene on campus, and one night, after I'd had a few drinks—something else I had refused to do in high school—a good-looking guy I hardly knew asked me to go upstairs with him. I don't remember much about that night except that it was awful. It was also the beginning of a horrible downhill slide in my life.

"I cast off all the prohibitions of my childhood beliefs and plunged into the party scene with reckless abandon. Mom and Dad could tell something was wrong when I went home over Christmas break, but I covered fairly well. Then I got my grades—I couldn't cover them. I had gone from an A student to academic probation in a few months' time. If I didn't pull up my grades during second semester, my first year of college would be my last.

"I went back to school after the break and immediately fell into the same patterns of partying and promiscuity. Then one night some friends asked me to go with them to hear a campus lecturer discussing the influence of supernatural spirits upon human beings. Once we got there, it didn't take me long to figure out that the guy was a Christian, and I almost got up and walked out. But he was talking about how demonic spirits attacked the human mind and slowly eroded a person's faith.

"The longer I listened, the more it sounded as though he was talking about me. I stayed for the entire lecture and listened intently to the question-and-answer session afterward. The guy answered a lot of my own questions. One thing he said really struck me. He said whenever you feel those deep-seated doubts about God plaguing your mind, recognize those as a demonic attempt to get you to disobey God. He said, 'Speak out loud and tell the demons to keep quiet. Then reaffirm your faith in God.'

"Later that night, I went back to my room, knelt down by my bed, and for the first time in ages, I prayed. I repented of my sins and asked God to forgive me and to change me. I started reading the Bible again. I also took that speaker's advice. Whenever I was tempted to doubt God—either intellectually, spiritually, or morally—I'd speak aloud, like Jesus did, and say, 'Satan, get behind me'; then I'd say, 'Jesus, I may not understand this, but I believe in You and I trust You, no matter what.'

"An amazing thing happened. As I rejected the devil's negative ideas and declared my faith in Jesus Christ, my doubts disappeared. The Word of God came alive to me in a fresh way, and I started seeing things in Scripture that I had never before seen. It hasn't all happened overnight; still, slowly but surely, I've been getting back my confidence in Christ. I'm convinced that the devil was using my doubts in an attempt to destroy my life here on earth and my future with Jesus in heaven."

Shannon's story illustrates the third important rule of spiritual warfare:

3. Never, ever feel that you need to defend God.

That's what Eve tried to do when she entered into a conversation with the devil. Certainly you need to know what and why you believe. Furthermore you should never back off from bearing witness for Christ, even if it costs you in the eyes or your family, friends, or coworkers. The apostle Peter wrote these encouraging words:

> Who is there to harm you if you prove zealous for what is good? But even if you should suffer for the sake of righteousness, you are blessed. AND DO NOT FEAR THEIR INTIMIDATION, AND DO NOT BE TROUBLED, but sanctify Christ as Lord in your hearts, always being ready to make a defense to everyone who asks you to give an account for the hope that is in you, yet with gentleness and reverence.
>
> —1 PETER 3:13–15

Eve probably thought she was doing a good thing by sticking up for God in the face of the devil. "No, sir!" she said to Satan. "You've got it all wrong. God said we can eat any of the fruit around here except the fruit from the tree that's in the middle of the garden. God said if we eat that fruit we will die—whatever that means" (my paraphrase of Genesis 3:2–3).

Poor Eve. She didn't realize that God was not threatened by the devil's derelict accusations. But she was. It's easy to second-guess and to be critical of Eve, looking back with the benefit of time and the rest of biblical revelations. But she had no idea how deadly it could be to fool around with the devil.

She did know God, though, and everything she knew about Him told her that He was a good, loving God. The best thing she could have done when Satan questioned God's motives would have been to say, "I don't know who you are or what you are, but I refuse to listen to this nonsense. God is God, and He is good. Even if I don't understand right now, if He said not to eat that fruit, I know it is for my own good. So shut your mouth, take your doubts, and get out of here."

Most Christians are too kind when the devil attempts to plant doubts in their minds. In words or thoughts, they seem to say something such as, "Well, thank you, Mr. Satan, for that interesting idea. It doesn't really line up with what I know about God, but I will certainly consider your suggestion."

That's pure poppycock. Don't be nice to the devil. Tell him off. Tell him to keep quiet and go back to hell or wherever Jesus sends him.

Don't worry about offending the devil. The devil is not a gentleman. Unfortunately you can't hurt his feelings. You won't bruise his ego to the point that he will not come back to see you again. Too bad.

Practice these words: "Keep quiet, you devil!" Go ahead; say them aloud, and when the devil or his demons begin knocking on the doors of your heart and mind, speak those words to them.

Unfortunately Eve was much too gracious when Satan began casting doubts upon God's goodness. She opened the door, and before she knew it, the devil had talked her into denying everything she believed to be true. It could happen to any one of us, if we deny God's Word. That's what happened to Amanda.

Chapter Five

WHO DO YOU THINK YOU ARE?

WHEN I FIRST met Amanda, she was the perfect embodiment of the tall, blonde, blue-eyed beauty queen. She had just won her first in a series of local pageants leading to the nationally televised finale. It's easy to think that most women who enter such events have fairly strong self-images. Amanda was the opposite.

Her father frequently poked fun at her because she was tall and awkward as a child, calling her names such as "Beanpole" and "Stringbean." Consequently when she looked into the mirror, she didn't see a beautiful, early bloomer. All she saw was a freak who was bigger than most of her female friends.

In junior high boys began to notice her...for all the wrong reasons. She often heard their loud, lewd comments about her fully developed body, and her face blushed with embarrassment.

"Why did God make me so ugly?" she lamented to her mom.

"That's not true, Amanda," her mom tried to console her. "You are beautiful."

"Yep. A little big but beautiful," her dad added playfully, not realizing the negative impact his words were having upon his daughter.

A teacher first suggested that Amanda enter a local beauty pageant. Amanda entered and won. For a few wonderful minutes while on the platform, she felt beautiful. That began Amanda's obsession with entering beauty contests. Although she didn't realize it at the time, in each of the pageants she was subconsciously attempting to win her father's favor as well as the crown. While others raved about her poise, charm, intelligence, and beauty, every time Amanda looked into a mirror, she saw a gangling teenage girl and heard her dad's negative words.

Amanda became a Christian, but she never really trusted God as her heavenly Father, and she never really felt accepted in His eyes. She said honestly, "I want to love God and believe that He loves me, but I can't."

That's all the forces of hell needed to hear. Amanda came under the devil's attack and began to have terrible nightmares in which she saw a creature that looked similar to her father screaming at her, "You are so ugly!" Why don't you just kill yourself?" Night after night Amanda awakened in a cold sweat. She'd look at herself in the mirror and feel a strong urge to take a razor and cut her beautiful face into ribbons. Fortunately she resisted the temptation. But it took more than a year of prayerful counseling and deliverance sessions before Amanda was free of the demonic influences and able to accept herself as precious to her heavenly Father.

If you are going to defeat the demons that assault your self-image, it is vital that you know and believe what God's Word says His attitude is toward you. The Bible says God loves you, and He proved it by giving the life of His only Son, Jesus, to purchase your deliverance from the devil. Furthermore, long before you were even born, long before the earth was formed, God loved you and had in mind a marvelous design for your life. While you were in your mother's womb—actually before you were even conceived by your parents—God put His stamp of approval upon you.

King David, an insightful poet and songwriter, put it this way in a song of praise and thanks to our Creator:

> You made all the delicate, inner parts of my body and
> knit me together in my mother's womb. Thank you for
> making me so wonderfully complex! Your workman-
> ship is marvelous—how well I know it. You watched
> me as I was being formed in utter seclusion, as I was
> woven together in the dark of the womb. You saw me
> before I was born. Every day of my life was recorded in
> your book. Every day was laid out before a single day
> had passed.
>
> —PSALM 139:13–16, NLT

Did you notice the wonderful truth of that Scripture passage?
Regardless of your appearance, talents, abilities, or any other
physical characteristic, your heavenly Father loves you. He created you as His own unique masterpiece. You are of inestimable
value to God because you have been handcrafted by Him as an
expression of His immeasurable greatness. The Bible says, "We
are His workmanship, created in Christ Jesus for good works,
which God prepared beforehand so that we would walk in them"
(Eph. 2:10).

In other words, a good God created you to do good things
with your life for His glory. He made you, He loves you, and
He wants the best for you. That is the consistent witness of
God's Word concerning His attitude toward you. Unfortunately
Amanda allowed the devil to distort that truth, causing her to
violate the fourth rule of spiritual warfare:

4. Never, ever deny God's Word!

Adam and Eve first violated this rule back in the Garden of
Eden. When Satan saw that Eve's confidence in God's goodness had been shaken, he became even bolder in his attack upon
her. He blatantly denied the authority of God's Word. You can
almost hear him sneering, "You surely will not die!" (Gen. 3:4).
The devil was lying again. God had specifically told Adam and

Eve that if they tasted of the forbidden fruit, they would die (Gen. 2:17). Now the devil was attempting to get Eve to doubt God's Word and the serious consequences disobedience would bring.

He tries to do the same thing to you and me. Once we concede God's goodness, Satan encourages us to take the next short step to doubting and disbelieving God's Word. One of Satan's favorite tricks is suggesting, "God didn't really mean that." When we doubt God's Word, it becomes easy to believe that the Bible is "just another book." You tend to think, "Yes, God may speak to me through this book, but then He might speak to me through *Reader's Digest* or *Playboy* or *Cosmopolitan* too."

That's why the most important battles in spiritual warfare will not be won by casting demons out of possessed people. The critical arena, and the most bitterly contested territory, is the battle for your mind. You must defeat the devil in this battle if you ever hope to win the war for other people's souls (as well as your own). How can you do that? How can you resist demonic attacks against your mind?

A good place to start is 2 Corinthians 10:3–5. Here the apostle Paul writes: "For though we walk in the flesh, we do not war according to the flesh, for the weapons of our warfare are not of the flesh, but divinely powerful for the destruction of fortresses. We are destroying speculations and every lofty thing raised up against the knowledge of God, and we are taking every thought captive to the obedience of Christ."

Paul is saying that even though we live in our physical bodies, our weapons of spiritual warfare are not physical but spiritual. The smartest, strongest, or richest person on earth doesn't stand a chance of defeating the devil without God's supernatural power. On the other hand, God's weapons are vastly more powerful than the devil's, and when properly used in the name of Jesus, they can destroy any demonic fortress you encounter.

That's God's part in the battle, but notice what your primary concern is in this matter. According to verse 5 you are to take "every thought captive to the obedience of Christ." In other words, you are to control your mind in such a way that your thought life is pleasing to Christ. That's why it is so important to guard your mental input. You need to be especially careful what movies, television shows, or music videos you watch, and what you read and the music you listen to.

It is no secret that two powerful influences upon our minds are movies and music. Put the two together in a music video format, and the message comes across with even more force. Is it any wonder, then, that the devil has gone to such great pains to demonize so much of today's music and so many of the movies playing in theaters, on network and cable TV, and the Internet?

The devil is not a dolt. He knows if he can convince you to let down the defenses of your mind, it won't be long before he wraps his red-hot fingers around your heart. On the other hand, if you win the day-to-day battles for your mind, you will eventually win the war. Sadly that is precisely the battle that Eve lost in Genesis 3 when she violated the fifth rule of spiritual warfare:

5. Never, ever doubt God's motives.

Eve took the next step toward destruction when she allowed the devil to talk her into doubting that God wanted the best for her. This was a direct attack upon God's character. In response to Eve's answer to Satan's question, the devil first contradicted God's Word. Then Satan said, "For God knows that in the day you eat from it your eyes will be opened, and you will be like God, knowing good and evil" (Gen. 3:5).

Did you notice the double whammy the enemy lays on Eve? First of all, he insinuates that God is holding out on her. He hints that there are all sorts of pleasures she has never experienced because that "big, bad God" of hers doesn't want her to know about them.

The devil has probably spoken something similar to you from time to time. He says, "How can you be so narrow-minded? Your attitudes toward sex and marriage are outdated. Sex is good; it's natural. You have strong desires. Do you mean to tell me that God gave you those desires and now He tells you not to express them? Come on, quit being such a prude.

"Drugs? Alcohol? Prescription medications? Listen, you have so much stress on you; how are you supposed to make it if you don't escape once in a while? Don't worry. You won't get addicted. You're too smart for that.

"Materialism? Sure, you need to save your money, and of course you can toss a few bucks in the church offering plate once in a while, but come on. You need a new, larger-screen TV. No wonder your friends don't want to hang out at your house. And listen, while you are at the mall, do something about your wardrobe, will you? You're dressing like your mom and dad!"

Satan suggests an entire array of pleasures, all of which imply, "There's a whole lot more to life than what you are experiencing—merely going to church, reading your Bible, and living that boring Christian life. God is keeping back the best stuff from you." Beyond that Satan makes it sound so easy to obtain life's "goodies."

"Look," he says, "I'm not asking you to deny Jesus; I'm just telling you that if you listen to me, I can get you things He won't give you. Nobody will know the difference. I'll never tell."

The second part of the devil's double whammy is even more seductive: "You will be like God." To the person who has already begun to doubt God's goodness, His Word, and His motives, Satan's suggestion makes perfect sense. "That's it! I can still be a Christian, but this is a new age. I don't have to be bound by the traditions of the past. I don't have to live my life according to some book, most of which I've never read, or if I have, never understood. God isn't just in the church; He's in the rocks, in the trees. I see God in you. I see God in me. You are God; I am God..." Bingo!

Down through history, from Adam and Eve to Nebuchadnezzar to Shirley MacLaine to contemporary talk-show hosts, men and women have always wanted to be their own gods. You can hear expressions of that attitude all around you, and some of them sound so right.

- "I want to do my thing *my* way."
- "It's my life, and I'll do whatever I want."
- "It's my right."
- "Watch out for 'number one.'"
- "Nobody tells me what to do."
- "I am my own person."
- "Stand tall, take up for yourself."
- "It's my body; it's my right to choose for myself."

But as Nebuchadnezzar already knows, and Shirley is sure to find out—as well as all who worship the god of self—there is only one God...and you and I are not Him!

Can you believe this? Satan was now tempting Eve with the exact sin that got him cast out of heaven in the first place. Remember? Lucifer wanted to be "like the Most High" (Isa. 14:14), so he rebelled against the Lord. Now there he was in the Garden of Eden dangling that same lie in front of Eve: "You will be like God" (Gen. 3:5).

Sadly the lie still seduces many of us today. The devil whispers in our ears, "You can be your own god," and although we know where that sort of thinking originates and where it leads, we say, "Well, maybe I can be a Christian and still live the way I want. Maybe I can do what I want and hope that it fits in with what God's Word says."

Let's quit kidding ourselves. There can be only one Lord of your life and mind. Jesus, Satan, or your self cannot all occupy the same throne. You must choose every day who will be God in your life.

The Old Testament prophet Elijah cut straight to the chase when he told the people of God, "How long will you hesitate between two opinions? If the LORD is God, follow Him; but if Baal, follow him" (1 Kings 18:21). Perhaps, if the prophet were speaking specifically to our generation, he might say something such as, "Make up your mind. If God is God, then let's serve Him. But if you want to be your own god, serve yourself. Keep in mind, however, where that self-exaltation got Lucifer and where it will ultimately take you if you insist upon pursuing that path."

Eve had almost reached the point of no return. She could still turn back. She could break off with the devil by calling out to God and asking Him for help, guidance, or clarification of His Word and His will. But she didn't. She allowed her eyes to focus on the forbidden fruit. After all, it looked *so* good.

Chapter Six

PASSING THE POINT
OF NO RETURN

LESS THAN A mile beyond the tranquil waters that flow beneath the Grand Island Bridge toward Niagara Falls is an infamous place that every boater fears: the point of no return. Once a boat has gone beyond this point, the power of the current increases exponentially, sweeping everything in its path toward an inevitable, horrifying, pounding slam-dunk onto the rugged rocks one hundred sixty feet below. Only a miracle can save a person once he or she has passed the point of no return. James Honneycut and two young friends of his, Roger Woodward, age seven, and Deanne Woodward, seventeen, learned that lesson the hard way.

The Honneycuts and Woodwards were having a marvelous day boating on the Niagara River well above the Grand Island Bridge. James Honneycut knew the river well, and he would never think of doing anything foolish that might jeopardize the safety of his family or friends. Nevertheless, just for fun, he decided to turn off the boat's engine, lie back in the sun, and drift a while. He had done something similar many times before and never experienced any danger.

On this day, however, James Honneycut allowed the boat to drift too far. He noticed the Niagara River becoming choppier, a clear warning sign that rough rapids lay ahead. Quickly

James pulled the crank on the boat's engine. Everyone on board breathed a sigh of relief when the motor roared to a start.

But as Honneycut attempted to steer the boat back upriver out of the rough water, to their stark terror the boaters discovered that the power of the rushing current had become too strong for their boat's engine. They were being swept helplessly toward the falls. Courageously Honneycut kept fighting the currents, pointing their craft into the ever-increasing rapids, first one way, then another. But his efforts were to no avail. The rapids tossed the tiny boat around as though it were a Ping-Pong ball.

As the thrashing river whipped the boaters toward Niagara's cataracts, their craft suddenly crashed into a large rock, splintering the boat. Had Honneycut and the Woodward kids seen it in time, they might have been able to reach out and grab onto the rock; they could have been saved. Instead the rock was their final undoing in their tumultuous trip. It shattered the boat, leaving the group to fend for themselves in their losing battle against the mighty Niagara.

Wearing only swimming suits and life preservers, Deanne, Roger, and James ricocheted across the rapids, being alternately sucked deeply beneath the foam, banging into sharp-edged rocks below, and then being rocketed back out into the current. The rapids swept Deanne near the shoreline of the infamous Terrapin Point on the American side of the 161-foot-high Horseshoe Falls. John Hayes, a visiting sightseer, saw the young woman smashing through the white-foamed rapids.

Risking his own life, he jumped the fence, ran across the slippery rocks to the edge of the turbulent river, and within a few feet from the crest of the falls, he reached out and grabbed Deanne by her hair. While the water ravenously attempted to rip her out of his grasp, the man struggled to maintain his footing and hold on to the young woman. Finally, with the assistance of another man who risked his life to help, Hayes was able to pull her bloody, exhausted body out of the current and onto the slippery rocks, saving her life.

The young woman's brother wasn't quite so lucky. The powerfully pounding water pitched Roger over the center of Niagara Falls. Miraculously, perhaps because the boy was so light-of-weight, the water whipped him away from the rock wall behind the crashing cataracts and beyond the dangerous rocks below the falls. He survived and was rescued by crew members aboard the *Maid of the Mist* sightseeing tour boat.

James Honneycut, however, plunged over the precipice and perished beneath the falls. His broken, battered body, apparently bludgeoned by the rushing water against the huge rocks jutting out below Niagara Falls, was found downriver three days later. He tragically perished—and endangered the lives of his friends—because he had drifted too long and had unwittingly crossed the point of no return.[1]

EVE'S THREE MISTAKES

Eve was right there at the point of no return. If she lingered one moment longer, she was going to be sucked over the brink by the devil's deception. "Eve! Get out of there! Eve! Don't do it!" all creation cried. But it was too late. Her eyes were locked onto that fruit like a computer-guided "smart bomb." And the next sound creation heard was a cosmic explosion.

Eve made three devastating mistakes in her dealing with the enemy's deception. Unfortunately we've all repeated Eve's errors in our own lives.

1. She looked and kept on looking.

In the type of society in which we live, it is certain that we are going to see evil things we do not intend to see and hear things we do not desire to hear. That's just reality. But we don't have to dwell upon those things that we know are counterproductive to our faith in Jesus Christ. Granted, sometimes crazy things just happen, things we didn't plan for or intend.

Once I was on an airplane and wanted to use the restroom. I walked casually toward the rear of the plane and spied one of the restrooms with the "vacant" sign showing on the door. I turned the handle, whipped open the door, and found myself standing face-to-face with a woman who looked as though she were about to sit down on the commode. I'm not sure which of us was more shocked, but for one of the few moments in my life, I was literally speechless.

Finally after a second or two, but what seemed like an eternity to me and probably longer to her, I blurted, "Uh, sorry!" and slammed the door. I returned to my seat, buried my head in a magazine, and suffered in silence until we arrived at our destination. No way was I going to walk down that aisle again!

When I think about that wacky episode, I cannot remember what the woman looked like. If you offered me all the money in the world to identify her, I would be unable to do it. Why? Because I responded immediately to what I had recognized as a wrong situation. I hadn't taken a course on "What to Do When Confronted With a Near-Naked Woman in an Airplane Restroom." I instinctively shut the door. I didn't stand there ogling the woman once I realized what had happened. Nor did I say, "Well, my, my; fancy meeting you here. Do you come here often?"

No, my response was simply a reflex action: *Oops! This is wrong. Slam the door.* I didn't have to pray about it or repent over it. All I had to do was slam the door.

Admittedly I haven't always responded so nobly or so quickly. But that's what most of us need to do more often when confronted by potentially compromising or sinful situations. Don't mull those images over in your mind; slam the door before the devil gets an opportunity to stick his foot in the doorway.

Eve didn't do that. Instead she looked at the forbidden fruit and kept on looking until she allowed her mind to fantasize about how good it would be. She could imagine how it would feel to touch the forbidden fruit, to hold it in her hands, to taste it with her tongue. No doubt, the fruit probably had a pleasant fragrance to it as well. Scripture says Eve "saw that the tree was good for food, and that it was a delight to the eyes, and that the tree was desirable to make one wise" (Gen. 3:6).

Satan was seducing Eve physically, emotionally, intellectually, and spiritually. Physically the attraction of the fruit and Eve's desire for it began to overwhelm her resistance. Emotionally she saw that the fruit was a delight to the eyes. Intellectually she looked at the fruit with all its potential to make her wise. Spiritually she knew nothing was innately wrong with the fruit; it was good for food. But it was forbidden fruit—fruit outside the will of God for Eve's life.

Suddenly, as Eve's senses were aroused, all of God's words to her seemed to go out the window. She wanted what she wanted, and she wanted it now. She reached her hand toward the tree.

2. Eve willfully disobeyed God.

Eve knew better. Yet "she took from its fruit and ate" (Gen. 3:6). Can you imagine what she must have been thinking as she bit into that fruit? Perhaps she felt liberated at last. Now she could choose her own lifestyle. She would soon know all about good and evil. She would be wise. Most importantly, now she could be her own god.

As the fruit slid down Eve's throat, she may have fleetingly wondered whether or not she was going to die, as God had said (Gen. 2:17). Maybe she thought, "Mmm-mmm, that was good.

And look, I'm still alive. I haven't had any noticeable negative effects from eating the fruit. In fact, I feel fantastic!"

That's the way the devil's devices are designed to work. At first everything seems delicious and delightful; in the long run sin will kill you. In the end sin brings nothing but disillusionment, death, and destruction.

3. She shared her sin.

Have you ever noticed that when somebody has a bad habit he or she wants to share it with you? "Have a beer." "Care for a cigarette?" "Want some marijuana? Come on, it won't hurt you." Sin is social; it always seeps out into society. Like buried toxic waste products, it has a tendency to come bubbling to the surface when you least expect it.

Moreover, most people who know they are guilty of sin want somebody else to experience it along with them. After all, if you sin with them, then they don't have to feel quite so guilty about their own rejection of God's Word or His ways. That's what motivates much of the so-called "gay rights" movement and the "abortion rights" activists. Beneath all the rhetoric about "rights" and "freedom" is an age-old human habit: people are attempting to rationalize their sin by seeking to involve somebody else.

That's what Eve did. No sooner had she willfully sinned against God (and against herself), the Bible says "she gave also to her husband with her, and he ate" (Gen. 3:6). That's one of the worst aspects of sin. Few people keep sin to themselves for long. Sin craves company, and it is contagious. Consequently sin not only hurts the person who has made a conscious decision to commit it, but sin also hurts everyone around the sinner. That's why it is so foolish to talk about a sinful affair in which nobody gets hurt. Somebody *always* gets hurt by sin, and usually more than one person is affected.

You have to wonder where Adam was while the devil was

deceiving his wife. The Bible doesn't say. For all we know, he may have been standing right there beside Eve the entire time. We have no record of his objecting when Eve gave him the forbidden fruit.

A case could easily be made that Adam was even more culpable than Eve. After all, the devil deceived Eve, but Adam willfully walked right into sin with his eyes wide open and his conscience screaming like a siren. Sin is always a choice. It is an act of your will. Granted, some people seem to "fall" into sin. Others seem to be "sucked" into sin. Nevertheless sin is always the result of conscious decisions.

Maybe Adam looked at Eve after she had eaten of the fruit and thought, "Well, she looks OK to me. So far she's still upright. Maybe God was joking about that 'you will surely die' stuff." Many people feel that way. They blatantly flaunt the fact that they have sinned, saying, "See, God hasn't zapped me for sinning." Others are less vocal but equally as gleeful over their apparent escape from God's judgment. They think, "Ha! I did it, and I got away with it."

What these people fail to realize is that God doesn't always pour out immediate punishment for sin, but He always judges sin. No sinner goes unnoticed in heaven. Judgment is certain. It will come, maybe not today, perhaps not tomorrow, but it will come. Furthermore sin fractures our fellowship with God and always causes negative consequences, frequently even after the affair has been confessed and forgiven.

A friend of mine smoked a lot of marijuana during his teenage and college years. Since then he committed his life to Christ, repented of his sin, and is now a dynamic witness for Jesus. Unfortunately, because of his extensive drug usage as a young man, he became sterile. He and his wife have not been able to conceive children. God has blessed them, but they acknowledge a sense of pain because of sins from the past. Sin leaves indelible marks upon our lives.

SIX CONSEQUENCES OF ADAM AND EVE'S SIN

In Adam and Eve's case some of the consequences of their sin were immediate while others were more long-term. First, sin changed Adam and Eve's attitude about themselves. The Bible says, "Then the eyes of both of them were opened, and they knew that they were naked" (Gen. 3:7). More than their physical eyes were opened; their "spiritual eyes" were opened as well. They truly began to see the awful difference between good and evil.

It is interesting to note that the Bible calls attention to their nakedness. Before they sinned, Adam and Eve "were both naked and were not ashamed" (Gen. 2:25). But after they had disobeyed God, they recognized the vulnerability of their situation (Gen. 3:7). They felt exposed in more ways than one and felt compelled to cover themselves.

Second, sin changed their attitude toward God. Scripture says, "They heard the sound of the LORD God walking in the garden in the cool of the day, and the man and his wife hid themselves from the presence of the LORD God among the trees of the garden" (Gen. 3:8).

How refreshing it must have been, after a good day's work, to walk and talk with the Creator in the cool of the day. But when Adam and Eve sinned, the last person they wanted to see that evening was the Lord. Instead they quickly tried to hide from His presence. People have been doing that ever since. When we sin, we have only two choices: either confess and repent or run and hide from God's presence.

Third, Adam and Eve's sin changed God's relationship to man. He still loved them just as much as before, but sin separated Adam and Eve from the intimate fellowship they had freely enjoyed with God. It also meant, because He is true to His Word, that He would judge Adam and Eve. There was a price to pay for their disobedience. God drove Adam and Eve out of the Garden of Eden (Gen. 3:24). God does not take sin lightly—even if we do. He doesn't say, "I know you disobeyed Me, but it's no big deal." Nor does He say, "You couldn't help yourself." Sin may not seem serious to some people, but it is definitely a big deal in God's sight. He hates it.

Fourth, the serpent was cursed (Gen. 3:14) due to its role as an agent of the devil in Adam and Eve's demise. We don't know what the serpent was like before the fall. Maybe snakes stood upright and were friendly creatures. Regardless, as part of God's judgment of this sin, the serpent was cursed and caused to crawl on its belly. Subsequently throughout history snakes have been used to represent evil. To most people snakes are repulsive.

Fifth, in some ways the earth itself was cursed because of Adam and Eve's sin. God said to Adam:

> Cursed is the ground because of you; in toil you shall eat of it all the days of your life. Both thorns and thistles it shall grow for you; and you shall eat the plants of the field; by the sweat of your face you shall eat bread, till you return to the ground, because from it you were taken; for you are dust, and to dust you shall return.
>
> —Genesis 3:17–19

God was not saying that everyone who lives would be a farmer; He was telling Adam that he was going to have to work hard to eke out a living from the land. Perhaps, had Adam and Eve never sinned, everything they needed would have been continually and bountifully provided for them in the garden. But now they were going to have to spend the majority of their days on earth struggling simply to survive.

Possibly at this point some of the animals turned hostile to man, or perhaps it merely seemed that way to Adam and Eve now that they could see the potential for evil in all that God had originally created as good. Human beings' indifferent attitude toward the environment could probably be traced to this point as well. Now rather than regarding the earth as a magnificent gift from God to be cultivated and cared for, it became something to be used for selfish gratification. It will be that way until Jesus returns and restores Earth to its original splendor— or better! No wonder, years later, the apostle Paul wrote:

> For the anxious longing of the creation waits eagerly for the revealing of the sons of God. For the creation was subjected to futility, not willingly, but because of Him who subjected it, in hope that the creation itself also will be set free from its slavery to corruption into the freedom of the glory of the children of God. For we know that the whole creation groans and suffers the pains of childbirth together until now.
>
> —ROMANS 8:19–22

In the meantime we should do our best to care for our environment, becoming good ecological stewards of the resources the Lord has given to us. At the same time we must recognize that God intended for mankind to rule over the earth (Gen. 1:26), and that dominion has never been rescinded. We are not to worship the earth, but we are to worship the One who created it and us.

The sixth and, in many ways, most damaging result of Adam and Eve's sin was death. Although it grieved God's loving heart, He held true to His Word. He had warned Adam and Eve not to eat the forbidden fruit, or they would die. Adam and Eve disobeyed God; they ate the fruit from the tree in the middle of the garden, and men and women have been dying ever since. Even though God didn't zap Adam and Eve with a lightning bolt the moment they ate of the forbidden fruit, in a sense, they died right then. Their sin separated them from the life of God, and without God, a person is dead.

STOMPING SNAKES

What does all this have to do with spiritual warfare? Simply this: by disobeying God, Adam and Eve walked right into Satan's trap. No doubt the devil had been looking for some way to get back at God since the day he and his demons were cast out of heaven.

More significantly God had given Adam and Eve authority to subdue and rule over the earth (Gen. 1:26–28), and the devil wanted it. Quite possibly Adam and Eve were still naïve concerning the tremendous gift God had given them; they didn't realize what they had, but Satan certainly understood the value of their authority. Remember, at one time God had delegated a great measure of authority to Lucifer. But when Lucifer misused his delegated authority, God removed it from him and cast him out of heaven.

Imagine Satan's mouth watering when he saw the amazing amount of power God placed in the hands of Adam and Eve. From the moment Adam took his first breath, the devil and his demons probably began plotting how they could usurp Adam's God-given authority. The forbidden fruit posed the perfect opportunity.

When Satan deceived Eve, and then both she and Adam disobeyed God by eating the forbidden fruit, the first couple unwittingly handed over their God-given authority to the devil, and he became the god of this world. They didn't know it, but they had traded a diamond for a lump of coal.

The devil and his demons probably would have had a huge celebration except for one thing. Right in the middle of all the doom, despair, and cursing of Genesis 3, God proclaimed some previews of coming attractions. He said to the serpent:

> And I will put enmity between you and the woman,
> and between your seed and her seed; he shall bruise you
> on the head, and you shall bruise him on the heel.
> —GENESIS 3:15

This promise of God is the *protoevangelium,* the first prophecy of the gospel of Jesus Christ and His ultimate victory over Satan. Notice the Lord said that Satan would bruise Jesus's heel, but Jesus would stomp on the serpent's head. The word used here for *bruised* literally means "to crush." One of the best cinematic interpretations of this was the opening scene of the movie *The Passion of the Christ,* when the slithering snake in the garden gets crushed.[2] All of this would come about through "the seed of the woman"; in other words, through the future generations yet to be born.

The devil well understood the implications of this divine declaration. Basically God was telling him, "You think you have won a major victory here, but one day you are going to get what is coming to you—and it won't be pretty." Satan may not have understood how his head was going to be crushed, but he realized it had something to do with the babies that were to be born to the woman. Satan knew that one of those kids was the key to his destruction.

Unquestionably that is why Satan has targeted innocent babies throughout history. From the ancient customs of child sacrifice in Old Testament times to the slaughter of infants at the birth of Jesus to attacks against children by means of abortion, child abuse, drug addiction, child pornography, incest, starvation, and a host of other atrocities, Satan has always exhibited an especially evil propensity for destroying children.

Most of us learned a song somewhere along the line that

says, "Jesus loves the little children, all the children of the world." That's true. What is equally true is that Satan hates those same children.

Throughout history, as recorded in the Old Testament, Satan attempted to discover and destroy the baby who would one day crush his head. Author Dean Sherman believes from a spiritual warfare perspective, the Old Testament can be summed up in two statements:

1. It is the historical record of God bearing the seed of the woman through the nation of Israel to bring Jesus Christ into the world.

2. It is the history of Satan's attempts to corrupt and destroy the seed that would bruise his head.[3]

But then one day a baby boy was born in Bethlehem, and the beginning of the end became obvious to Satan. Still, the devil blew it. Throughout Jesus's life Satan sought an opportunity to kill Him. When the Roman soldiers pounded the huge spikes into Jesus's hands and feet, nailing Him to the cross, Satan most likely assumed the war was over and he had defeated God's plans to destroy him.

"Ha!" he may have boasted to his demonic friends. "God said I would bruise His heel, huh? I've bruised His entire body! Look at Him there, hanging on a cross. And that's the one who is supposed to crush my head? I guess we know who's boss now, don't we?"

Little did the devil know that as Jesus died on the cross, He was fulfilling His Father's plan to crush Satan's head and to set mankind free from the power of sin that began back in the Garden of Eden. In a sense Jesus was buying back with His blood what Satan had stolen from Adam and Eve and every person since then.

But Jesus went even further than that. The apostle Paul explains, "When He had disarmed the rulers and authorities, He made a public display of them, having triumphed over them through Him" (Col. 2:15). The rulers and authorities that Jesus disarmed were not physical, human beings. They were Satan's powers.

Beyond that, by dying on the cross and then rising from the dead three days later, just as He had prophesied, Jesus took away one of Satan's most powerful weapons, the threat of death. Now Jesus holds the keys to death and Hades. Jesus Himself declared, "I was dead, and behold, I am alive forevermore, and I have the keys of death and of Hades" (Rev. 1:18). The resurrection of Jesus Christ proved that Satan was defeated; he was powerless to stop Jesus from coming out of that grave.

Satan now knows that his days are numbered. Like a condemned criminal serving multiple life sentences, he has a "what have I got to lose" attitude. The devil knows that ultimately he can't win; he won't win. Jesus's crucifixion, burial, and resurrection guaranteed that. But Satan is determined to rob, kill, and destroy all that he can until the day he goes down in a flame of fire (Rev. 20:10). The only pleasure left for him is to somehow lure people away from trusting in the Lord. He does this by attempting to keep the gospel from being spread and by thwarting the progress of any person who truly wants to live for Jesus.

The result is what we know as spiritual warfare. The devil no longer wastes his time trying to storm the gates of heaven (although according to Revelation 12:10 he spends quite a lot of time before God accusing our brothers and sisters of horrible lies). Nor does the devil lob Scud missiles in the direction of the angels who are gathered around the throne of God.

No, the arena of the battle has changed. The battlefield is now this world, both in the air and on the ground, in your life and in mine. That's why it is so extremely important that you prepare yourself to fight back. You need to know how the devil is most likely to attack, what his strengths are, and what his weaknesses are. You are not fighting an ordinary foe; you're fighting a "madman" with no future and nothing more to lose. It's time to get ready.

Chapter Seven

THE DEVIL'S GAME PLAN

For TWENTY-ONE YEARS, every autumn Sunday afternoon, Tom Landry stood along the Dallas Cowboy sidelines, peering from beneath the brim of his trademark hat. Landry literally revolutionized the game of professional football with his intricate defenses and his lightning-fast, quick-hitting, strike-from-anywhere offensive strategies. Until 1989 he was the first and only coach of the Cowboys, leading them to an impressive 271 wins, 180 losses, and 6 ties during his tenure with the team. He was elected to the Pro Football Hall of Fame in 1990.

In his autobiography Tom Landry revealed one of the main secrets to his success as a football player and coach:

> I'd learned as a defensive back that it wasn't enough for me to react to the movement of the ball; by the time I saw where the ball was being thrown and tried to get there it would be too late to stop the play. My survival as a defensive player had forced me to "read" an offense, to anticipate what plays my opponents ran. Some of my ability was probably instinctive and enhanced by my analytical engineering education; but a lot of it came only after thousands of hours watching and dissecting game film.
>
> Eventually I learned that by watching or "keying" on players, on their movements, and the overall formation or positioning of the offensive players, I could consistently tell where the ball would be going. I no longer

had to react; I would anticipate the offense—sometimes breaking up even the most well-executed plays. That mind game—recognizing what the other team was wanting to do and stopping them from doing it—was the intriguing challenge of defensive football.[1]

On the other hand Landry realized that the best way to defeat a strong defense was to vary his offensive team's formations so often and with so many different plays the defense had less time to recognize how the Cowboys were going to hit them. Ordinarily Coach Landry didn't spend much time watching what his offensive team was doing. He was concentrating on what new obstacles the defensive team was placing in his way and planning his next move to get around the opposition. Landry explains:

> I always knew what play we had called; I didn't have to watch it. The only uncertainty was how the opposition reacted; it was their defense I needed to watch and analyze so I would know best how to counter it. And once a play ended, I never had time to react, immediately shifting focus to my game plan to decide what play I should send in next.[2]

In many ways spiritual warfare is similar to the way Tom Landry approached a football game. The "game" is between two teams, the church of Jesus Christ—of which you are a part if you genuinely know Jesus—and the demonic powers of darkness, coached by Satan himself. Two clearly delineated goals are already established, heaven and hell. Christ's team is meant to be moving toward the goal of heaven while attempting to keep Satan's team from making any serious incursions into the church's territory.

However, Satan's squad is blocking, tackling, and stunting the church's forward progress, and threatening to do even worse.

As the demonic force deploys its powerful offensive thrust, it is pushing the church backward, sending Christians reeling, stumbling over themselves, and putting up only a disabled, disorganized defense.

Worse yet, the demonic team doesn't play fair. They sneak across the line and listen to the church's signals while the church is in a huddle. They kick the Christians when they are down or when they are trying to get back on their feet after being knocked down. They constantly tell the referee lies about members of Jesus's team.

Perhaps the most insidious strategy of Satan's squad involves where they line up. Rather than standing in a straight line near midfield, waiting to kick or receive, the demons assemble right near the Christians' benches along the sidelines. They attempt to gang-tackle or trip any Christian who has the nerve to come off the bench, hoping to get onto the playing field. The demons learned long ago that they can "score" much more easily if they simply keep all those Christians off the field entirely.

Many Christian "players" have become so accustomed to being accosted every time they come off the bench that they have given up trying to get onto the field. Oh, sure; they still show up every week and dress for the game, but they merely hang around the sidelines talking with other members of the team about the glory days of yesteryear or those they believe are yet to come. They never get their uniforms dirty, they rarely work up a sweat, and they constantly watch the clock, hoping the game will end soon so they can get together afterward to rehearse strategies for the next week's big game. Usually such meetings are conducted at a popular local restaurant. Other team members simply want to get home and change into their more comfortable "street clothes."

Although the Christian team hasn't done so well on the field in recent years, the church has developed an outstanding array of cheerleaders. Men and women of all sizes, shapes, and abilities assemble weekly along the sidelines and cheer enthusiastically. They sing songs about the coach and about past triumphs. They carry their playbooks and sometimes even read them. The younger cheerleaders plan retreats in which they can get away from the intensity of the game for a while and have fun with their fellow cheerleaders. Some of the older cheerleaders engage in countless business meetings, discussing the price of everything from the popcorn in the pews…er, bleachers, to how much it will cost to recruit a new quarterback and some speedsters to whom he can pass or hand off the ball. It's all pretty much irrelevant, because the players rarely get off the sidelines anyhow.

It's really amazing that the spectators keep showing up to watch the games. Apparently they have become so enthralled by all the exciting activity on the sidelines, they have forgotten that the real action is supposed to take place on the field. The church of Jesus Christ has gotten so comfortable with this weird game that it has ignored the original goals espoused by the coach. Meanwhile the powers of darkness rip up and down the field in a rout.

Some may protest that this description is too harsh. Quite the contrary; if anything it is too kind. Numerous other parallels could be drawn between a football game and spiritual warfare. Unfortunately the battle between the church of the Lord Jesus Christ and powers of darkness is not a game; it is war. I wish we could talk about this subject in friendlier terms. I'd love to call it a "spiritual soap opera" or even a "spiritual reality show" or a "spiritual situational comedy" where whatever problem occurs is solved to everyone's satisfaction within thirty minutes to an hour, give or take a few commercials.

But the Bible describes our battle against the devil as war. Unlike most football games, soap operas, reality shows, and sitcoms, spiritual warfare is a live-and-death struggle, with eternal consequences hanging in the balance. It may literally mean the difference between heaven and hell for some people.

THE DEVIL'S STRATEGY

The first time Satan is specifically mentioned by name in the Bible is in 1 Chronicles 21:1. In this passage dealing with King David's foolish and unnecessary numbering of the people in Israel, we can see Satan's basic strategy revealed. He plans to deceive spiritual leaders so he can bring the name of God into disrepute.

Scripture says, "Then Satan stood up against Israel and moved David to number Israel" (1 Chron. 21:1). Satan tempted King David to conduct a census of his people. It seemed like an innocuous, even logical, thing to do. After all, every leader wants to know who his followers are, how many people are in the land he must protect, and how many soldiers are in his army. No doubt David never even suspected that this idea had been placed in his mind by the devil himself. Like Eve before him, the more David mulled it over in his mind, the more the sin made sense.

But what is so sinful about a census? In the United States a census is taken every ten years. It is a huge expense and an enormous undertaking, but it certainly doesn't seem to be sinful. What made David's census so dangerous?

Simply this: Although technically David's census was a legitimate thing for him to do, his reason for the census was wrong. David was beginning to take excessive pride in his military strength, his mighty army's fighting expertise, and he was forgetting that his real strength came from the Lord. Remember, this was the guy who as a boy had leveled a gigantic oaf named Goliath with just a few pebbles and a slingshot (1 Sam. 17:50). Now he was sliding into the trap of self-sufficiency, pride, and arrogance.

Even though David knew better, he allowed himself to trust

his own strength rather than God's. Mark it well: confidence in yourself apart from God will spell defeat in spiritual warfare every time.

Even Joab, King David's top military commander (a man not exactly known for his fine, upstanding morals), recognized the potential sinfulness of the census. He tried to diplomatically dissuade David from polling the people: "Joab said, 'May the LORD add to His people a hundred times as many as they are! But, my lord the king, are they not all my lord's servants? Why does my lord seek this thing? Why should he be a cause of guilt to Israel?'" (1 Chron. 21:3).

Whoa! Have you ever had a less mature Christian brother or sister question your motives? "Hey, I thought you trusted God. Why would you ever want to do a thing that looks shady?" Or, "Why would you want to go to that place or see that kind of a show or involve yourself in such an activity?" Or, "Why would you say a thing like that? I thought you were a Christian." Pay close attention when people question your motives. They may be trying to tell you something.

Despite Joab's reluctance, he carried out the king's command and conducted the census. But it displeased the Lord, and He punished Israel. When David realized the seriousness of his sin, he repented: "David said to God, 'I have sinned greatly, in that I have done this thing. But now, please take away the iniquity of Your servant, for I have done very foolishly'" (1 Chron. 21:8).

Notice that David took responsibility for his sin and repented. He didn't say, "The devil made me do it," nor did he try to pass the blame onto Joab. Despite the deception of the devil, David knew he was the one who had made the wrong choices. God forgave David, but the consequences of his sin cost the lives of seventy thousand men.

In this account, as in the record of Adam and Eve, we can see how the devil likes to work. He deceives the people of God into willfully disobeying, which in turn brings punishment from God.

"But that's not fair!" you might protest.

No, it is not, but as we've already noted, the devil doesn't fight fairly. Satan almost always starts his attack with deception. Perhaps that is why the apostle Paul warned, "But I am afraid that, as the serpent deceived Eve by his craftiness, your minds will be led astray from the simplicity and purity of devotion to Christ" (2 Cor. 11:3). Paul also mentions Satan's schemes in 2 Corinthians 2:11.

Once the devil finds an inroad to a person's life, Satan will often discard his tactics of subtle deception and attack in some more overt manner. That's what happened when the devil duped King David, the leader of God's people, into conducting the unnecessary census.

FOLLOW THE LEADER

Since Satan can be in only one place at a time, he likes to multiply his efforts by targeting spiritual leaders, attempting to topple them from their positions of influence and thus affecting a much larger number of people. His most effective tools in this battle seem to be sex, money, and pride, which often go hand in hand with power and position.

Satan knows that if he can deceive a Christian leader into compromising his or her integrity in any of these areas, the ripple effect of that leader's sin will spread far and wide. Unfortunately our generation is all too familiar with this strategy, as one high-profile Christian leader after another has fallen into disrepute. Ironically the church at large does little to help defend its leaders against these obvious and insidious attacks, expecting leaders to be strong enough to withstand temptations on their own.

It's not that leaders who succumb to these sins or any others cannot be forgiven, restored, and used again mightily in the kingdom of God. They can be. Their roles of leadership in the kingdom, however, will probably change radically. Maybe that's what James had in mind when he wrote, "Let not many of you become teachers, my brethren, knowing that as such we will incur a stricter judgment" (James 3:1).

God expects those who claim to represent Him before the public to do so with a holy integrity and humility. Furthermore it is not that pastors, teachers, evangelists, youth leaders, or political or business leaders who are Christians have an "in" with God; they simply have a wider sphere of influence than the person who is not so well known. Their words and examples affect the spiritual lives of more people; therefore, God holds them more accountable in their lifestyles.

As such we should pray for our spiritual leaders every day. And if you are in a position of spiritual servant-leadership, you should remind yourself often of the prophet Micah's words:

> He has told you, O man, what is good; and what does the LORD require of you but to do justice, to love kindness, and to walk humbly with your God?
>
> —MICAH 6:8

The words spoken by the prophet Amos sound similar, and you do not need to be a brilliant theologian or Bible scholar to figure out their meaning:

> Seek good and not evil, that you may live; and thus may the LORD God of hosts be with you, just as you have said!
>
> —AMOS 5:14

Unquestionably spiritual leaders who are attempting to serve the Lord encounter more opposition from Satan and his demonic assistants than lukewarm, casual believers. If you are "lukewarm," Jesus said, "I will spit you out of My mouth"

(Rev. 3:16). Satan simply plays a waiting game with those who are complacent about Christianity. Satan knows they will self-destruct. All he needs to do is make sure they don't repent and rekindle an "on-fire" relationship with Christ.

On the other hand Satan targets vibrantly alive Christians who are effectively living for Christ and witnessing about Him to others. That is no excuse for spiritual leaders who succumb to sin; they should know the opposition always "keys" on somebody who is doing something notable for the kingdom. In a football or basketball game, for example, the superstar is almost always double-teamed by the opposition. That is not a rationale for slacking off on the part of the star, nor does it cause the coach to take the quality player off the field. It is simply a given: the added pressure goes with the territory.

THE AIRPLANE STORY

One account of how Satan is targeting Christianity's spiritual leaders has gained almost mythological status. It is known as "the airplane story." When I first heard the tale, I regarded it as a good illustration but something that was probably spawned in the overactive imagination of an overzealous spiritual warrior.

I filed it in my mind alongside the perennial false accusations lodged against the Proctor & Gamble company when a group of sincere but misguided Christians asserted that the symbol on the company products had satanic origins. The Proctor & Gamble episode was tucked away neatly next to the myriad reports that crossed my desk alerting me to atheist Madalyn Murray O'Hair's supposed efforts to get the Federal Communications Commission (FCC) to take Christian radio and television programming off the air. Contrary to popular belief no such action was ever seriously proposed to or by the FCC.

Next to the O'Hair reports was my favorite outlandish overreaction to Satan's strategies by well-meaning Christians. In the mid-1980s an Ohio church youth group made national news when they destroyed a bunch of old "Mr. Ed" records because of the supposed satanic content of the phrase "A horse is a horse, of course, of course." Their contention was that when they played the talking horse's theme song backward, it was giving glory to Satan (not to mention what it did to their stereo needles— remember them?).

With such ridiculous overreactions popping up regularly, you can understand why I didn't take the airplane story seriously, especially when, like the nonexistent O'Hair efforts, the details of the story changed each time I heard or read it. Furthermore it always happened to somebody else. The people relating the story never personally knew the people involved (often a telltale sign of a "fish story").

But Dr. Ed Murphy, a professor of Bible and Missions at San Jose Christian College and a noted authority on the subject of spiritual warfare, asserts the airplane story is true. Whether this is the original incident or a copycat version, Dr. Murphy says the airplane story happened to a prayer partner of his.

Pat, Dr. Murphy's friend, was seated in the same row as a young man on board a flight out of San Jose. When it was time for the flight attendants to serve the meal (remember those?), Pat accepted hers, but the young man refused to eat, saying he was fasting. Dr. Murphy continues the story:

> "I overheard you tell the stewardess you are fasting," my friend said. "Then you must be a Christian."
> "No, I am a Satanist," was the reply.
> Pat was taken back by his remark. She did not know if she should look for another seat on the plane or what! She decided to stay where she was and engage the young man in conversation if he would. In fact, he was quite willing to talk of his faith and witness to the power of Satan.

In the course of the conversation, Pat asked him about the specific targets of his fasting and praying. (Such fasting and praying is a curse attempt, not humble supplication.) He said the targets were the leading churches and pastors in the San Jose area and two leading missions.[3]

I have heard this story and variations of it so many times now, even if Satan didn't dream up the idea, the devil has certainly capitalized on it. The most frequent reason given for the fasting of the Satanist is the destruction of the marriages, families, and homes of Christian leaders. I've heard stories told by devout Christians who report similar conversations held in restaurants, grocery stores, doctors' offices, and Laundromats. It would not surprise me to learn that these accounts are true. Satan knows that when a private citizen falls into sin, it may severely hurt that person and his or her family and friends. But when a Christian leader sins, it often brings the entire church of Jesus Christ into disrepute.

SATAN DESIRES TO DISHONOR GOD'S HOLY NAME

Slandering the name of God is the ultimate purpose for all of the devil's deception. In David's case, by deceiving the leader of God's people the devil succeeded in bringing shame upon the nation of Israel. Worse yet the sin was a reproach to God's name. What an insult to God for the leader of His people to trust an army more than Him! Moreover, by deceiving David, the devil also indirectly caused the people to come under God's judgment, and seventy thousand died as a result of the ripple effect of David's sin.

The Bible is replete with instances of Satan trying to sully the name of the Lord. All too often he succeeded. The only times he did not succeed were when God's people stood up and fought back. A good illustration of this can be found in 1 Samuel 11:1. Here we meet Nahash the Ammonite, who came up and besieged Jabesh-gilead, a town where many of God's people were living at the time.

You can almost imagine what kind of guy this Nahash was just from the sound of his name. He was your basic Hells Angels type of animalistic Ammonite. He was Mr. Tough Guy, Mr. Yuk. One day he came into town on his Harley (or motorized camel, or pimped-out '52 pickup goat), and everyone could tell Nahash was looking for a fight.

But God's people in Jabesh-gilead didn't want to fight, so instead they offered to make a deal with Nahash. They said, "Make a covenant with us and we will serve you" (1 Sam. 11:1). Obviously these guys were charter members of "The Jabesh-gilead Wimps for Jesus" club. By this compromising statement they were saying, "We don't want any trouble, Mr. Nahash; you just tell us what to do and we will serve you." How embarrassing! And that was the "fearless" response of the people of God to the advance of the enemy.

But Nahash wasn't buying it. After all, Nahash had come looking for a fight; he was cruisin' for some bruisin'. Consequently he wasn't excited about cutting a deal with the Wimps for Jesus. The enemy never comes merely to coerce compromising covenants from God's people. His purpose is to rob, to plunder, to kill, and to destroy.

Nevertheless Nahash agreed to play along with the people of Jabesh-gilead. Well, sorta. What he actually said was: "I will make it with you on this condition, that I will gouge out the right eye of every one of you, thus I will make it a reproach on all Israel" (v. 2).

Now what was Nahash going to do with all those right eyes? Was he going to open the Jabesh-gilead Eye Bank for People Who Are Blind in One Eye?" No! He said it himself: his sole purpose was to bring disgrace upon the people of God, and by doing so he would bring dishonor to the name of God.

The spiritual leaders (if that's what you can call them) of Jabesh said, "Give us seven days to think about it. If we can't find anybody to deliver us, we'll come out to you and you can poke our eyeballs out" (my paraphrase of verse 3). Nahash agreed. After all, he had nothing to lose.

Then God's people sent messengers to Gibeah, the town where the newly appointed first king of Israel, Saul, lived. The messengers told everyone about Nahash's challenge, "and all the people lifted up their voices and wept" (v. 4). When the people told their sad story to Saul, he didn't console them; he got mad. Really *mad*! The Scripture says, "Then the Spirit of God came upon Saul mightily when he heard these words, and he became very angry" (v. 6).

Too often we think that every time the Holy Spirit comes upon a person, He comes to bring peace. Not necessarily. When the Holy Spirit came upon Saul, he got angry—angry at this sin, angry at the intended insult against the name of the Lord.

How angry did Saul get? This angry: he took a pair of oxen, cut them into pieces, and mailed them off by messenger to various people all over Israel (v. 7).

Picture this: You're sitting down to the breakfast table in the morning when suddenly you hear a loud knock on the door. You answer and discover it is an overnight delivery service bringing a large box marked "Priority Delivery." You bring the heavy package into the kitchen and place it on the table. The other family members go wild.

"I want some!"

"Yeah, gimme some too. I want some!"

"Calm down," you say. "You don't even know what it is."

"I don't care, I want some."

Slowly you untie the heavy string wrapped around the package, and then pull open the flaps. In the box is a huge cow's head with a note stuck on one of his horns. The message says, "This will happen to your oxen if you don't come quickly! Signed, Saul."

The people came.

The Bible says, "Then the dread of the LORD fell on the people, and they came out as one man" (v. 7). Can you blame them? You and I probably would have come too, whether we wanted to fight or not. At least 330,000 men joined Saul in the fight against Nahash and the Ammonites. God's people struck down the enemy all morning long until Nahash and his followers were either scattered or destroyed.

Saul was wise enough to recognize the source of his army's strength. After the battle some of his overzealous followers wanted to snuff out some of their own people who had previously opposed Saul's leadership. They were really getting into this warfare thing. "But Saul said, 'Not a man shall be put to death this day, for today the LORD has accomplished deliverance in Israel'" (v. 13). Too bad that Saul did not maintain that sort of humility once he solidified his power base.

At that time, however, Saul understood that a Holy Spirit–inspired rage against the enemy was a good thing. It led to a righteous resolve to rally the people together to drive the enemy out of their town, which brought about God-honoring results.[4] That same pattern will help you defeat the devil in your life as well. But first let's look at where the real battle lines are drawn.

Chapter Eight

BATTLE STATIONS

IN SPIRITUAL WARFARE, as in any warfare, strategic areas—those considered vital to survival—must be heavily fortified to protect them against the attacks of the enemy. In war it is extremely important to prepare for the unexpected and to never underestimate the tenacity of your enemy. In the early months of World War II the British Empire failed to do both.

Most Americans remember the Japanese sneak attack upon Pearl Harbor, December 7, 1941, as the key element in Japan's master plan to conquer the Pacific. That same week, however, Japan also launched attacks against important United States outposts in the Philippines, Wake Island, Guam, and the British-held colonies of Malaya, Burma, and Hong Kong.

One of the most devastating blows was dealt to the peninsula of Malaya, a huge source of rubber and tin considered crucial by the Japanese if their war effort was to succeed. Malaya was defended by the strategic citadel of Singapore. The fortress at Singapore was built by the British in the 1920s and 1930s at a cost of more than $270 million. It was supposed to be the impregnable headquarters of the British fleet in the Pacific. The British considered the dense jungle behind Singapore to be virtually impassable, so they concentrated their efforts on defending against an attack from the sea. They brought in mammoth guns with barrels as large as fifteen inches in diameter and placed their heavy artillery array in cement and had it pointing out toward the ocean.

During the early days of World War II, the British posted eighty-five thousand men in Singapore to prepare for an "inevitable" naval attack. The British force had no tanks and no weapons to disable enemy tanks since they believed the jungle to be "impenetrable."

Unfortunately the British forgot to tell that to the Japanese, who attacked the peninsula by land from the north, rolling over the British in their Japanese tanks. When the Japanese reached the dense part of the Malayan jungle, they resorted to thousands of bicycles to transport their troops. Before long the bicycle tires went flat, but the tenacious enemy troops continued clanking forward on bare rims, hacking their way through the thick jungle with machetes as they went.

For seventy days they hacked, peddled, and clanked their way the length of the Malayan peninsula—a staggering distance of more than six hundred miles. When the overconfident British troops finally realized that they were, in fact, being attacked from behind—through the "impenetrable" jungle—it was too late. Their awesome fifteen-inch gun barrels that were set in cement could not be turned around to fire into the jungle, so they sat idle while the Japanese hacked their way into history. The Japanese bombardment began on February 7, 1942, and by February 15, the British surrendered the city of Singapore along with eighty-five thousand troops, who became prisoners of war.

There are two strategic areas that are both vital to your spiritual welfare and extremely vulnerable in spiritual warfare. They must be defended at all costs. Furthermore you must never become overconfident or complacent concerning these areas and never underestimate Satan's tenacity in attempting to destroy you through these "back doors." The two areas you must guard with your life are your mind and your heart. These are the places the devil most often attempts to attack, using his deceptive jungle warfare.

THE BATTLE FOR YOUR MIND

The truth cannot be overemphasized: some of the most important battles in spiritual warfare take place inside your head. But as we have already noted, the devil and his demons cannot read your mind or make you think a certain way on any subject. The devil's only power is to tempt. Satan and his assistants are masters at "suggesting" evil to your mind. When this happens, your response should be to reject the thought immediately.

A good example of this in Jesus's life occurred when He asked His disciples what the outside world was saying about Him. The disciples reported that some people were assuming that Jesus was John the Baptist, alive from the dead; others thought He might be Elijah, and still others said He was Jeremiah or one of the other prophets (Matt. 16:14). Then Jesus brought the issue into clearer focus for them: He continued by questioning them, "But who do you say that I am?" (v. 15).

There it is—the central question about Jesus. Everything the disciples did with Jesus, including the personal time they spent with Him as well as the miracles they witnessed everywhere they went with Him, was designed to bring them to this pivotal point. It is the turning point for any person when he or she truly answers Jesus's question, "But who do you say that I am?"

Peter, the most outspoken of the disciples, hit the nail right on the head when he answered, "You are the Christ, the Son of the living God" (v. 16). With those simple words the fisherman-turned-disciple uttered one of the most profound statements in human history. By acknowledging that Jesus was the Christ, Peter was saying, "Jesus, You are the Messiah; You are the one we've been watching and waiting for all these years; all of our hopes and dreams are wrapped up in You."

It was one of the climactic moments in Scripture when Jesus answered Peter, "Blessed are you, Simon Barjona, because flesh and blood did not reveal this to you, but My Father who is in heaven. I also say to you that you are Peter, and upon this rock I will build My church; and the gates of Hades will not overpower it" (vv. 17–18).

But then, just five verses later, after Peter had taken Jesus aside and protested about Jesus's discussion of His going to the cross (vv. 21–22), Jesus turned to Peter and said, "Get behind Me, Satan! You are a stumbling block to Me; for you are not setting your mind on God's interests, but man's" (v. 23).

Wait a minute. What happened? Had Peter suddenly denied his discipleship and become possessed by Satan? On the contrary, he was trying to protect Jesus from the awful future Jesus had just prophesied about Himself. Peter's thought, however, came right out of the pits of hell, and Jesus recognized it as such. It was the same tantalizing thought with which Satan had enticed Jesus during His temptations in the wilderness (Matt. 4:1–11): namely, that somehow or other Jesus could achieve the goals of God without suffering the pain of the cross. Jesus had rejected that thought when Satan had proposed it before, and He rejected it now when it came out of the mouth of one of His closest friends. That's why Jesus rebuked Peter so adamantly.

When the devil plants a thought in your mind that you know is contrary to the will of God, don't be afraid to rebuke that thought or the source. For instance, if your mind suddenly seems saturated with thoughts of suicide, illicit drugs, sex outside of marriage, becoming involved in occult activities, dishonest business practices, or any other thoughts that you know go against God's Word, immediately reject those ideas as from the devil. Speak aloud if you want: "Satan, get behind me. You don't have in mind the things of God but of men."

Once when I was speaking on this subject, a sincere young

man asked, "How in the world are we supposed to not think about something?"

Good question. It's the old pink elephant syndrome: when somebody tells you not to think of pink elephants, although you have never seen such an animal, your mind tries desperately to conjure up the image.

The only way you can *not* think about something is to change the subject. Dr. David Seamands, noted author and speaker, suggests blinking your eyes hard. It breaks your concentration.[1] Sweeping your hand across your forehead or shaking your head often helps as well, although you might feel rather silly doing so perpetually in your office, school, or home.

The important point to understand is you can't simply turn off thinking about evil; you have to "change the channel." Even after you have rejected Satan's seed-thoughts, you need to replace the negative thoughts with good thoughts. That's what the apostle Paul was talking about when he said, "Whatever is true, whatever is honorable, whatever is right, whatever is pure, whatever is lovely, whatever is of good repute, if there is any excellence and if anything worthy of praise, dwell on these things" (Phil. 4:8).

THE BATTLE FOR YOUR HEART OF HEARTS

The second area you must guard carefully is your heart. Nowadays we are accustomed to using the phrase, "I love you with all my heart," referring to our hearts as the fountain of our emotions. In the Bible, however, the heart meant much more than the source of mush-gushy sentiment. The heart was considered the center of the will. Out of it flowed a person's emotions, but beyond that the heart represented a person's *attitude*; thus the phrase "heart-attitude." Most of us wouldn't get too emotionally excited about someone telling us, "I love you with all my heart-attitude," but from a biblical standpoint, that would be a much firmer foundation upon which to build a relationship.

Jesus clearly saw the attitude of the person's heart and his or her outward actions as interrelated. To Jesus it was a two-way street. For example, He said, "You have heard that it was said, 'YOU SHALL NOT COMMIT ADULTERY'; but I say to you, that everyone who looks at a woman with lust for her has committed adultery with her already in his heart" (Matt. 5:27–28). Jesus was saying that lust in the mind and heart is basically the same as the physical act; to willfully harbor the heart-attitude of lust is as sinful as the act of adultery. The only thing lacking is opportunity.

Many men and women mistakenly assume that since Jesus equated the thought with the act, they may as well go ahead and commit immorality. Wrong. Although lustful thoughts lead to sin, they can be repented of, taken captive, and overcome without harming another individual. When you follow through with the thought and commit an immoral act, inevitably you will hurt somebody beside yourself. Granted, the sinfulness of the thought and deed can be equally damning, but the immediate repercussions and ramifications may be more severe.

Similarly Jesus taught His disciples, "For from within, out of the heart of men, proceed the evil thoughts, fornications, thefts, murders, adulteries, deeds of coveting and wickedness, as well as deceit, sensuality, envy, slander, pride and foolishness. All these evil things proceed from within and defile the man" (Mark 7:21–23). When Jesus talked about changing our hearts, He aimed directly at our attitudes.

WHAT AN ATTITUDE!

Have you ever heard it said of someone, "Boy, that person really has an attitude"? What do we mean by that comment? Usually it is a polite way of saying that person is proud or arrogant.

Furthermore most people are painfully familiar with the phrase, "He (or she) has a bad attitude." That statement usually implies that he or she is lazy, cocky, rude, disrespectful, or rebellious. Often this bad attitude is reflected in rebellion against parents or rebellion against those having spiritual, economic, or political authority.

Rebelling against God-ordained authority is a serious sin. In fact, when King Saul rebelliously disobeyed God's specific instructions given to him by the prophet Samuel, the prophet severely rebuked him: "For rebellion is as the sin of divination, and insubordination is as iniquity and idolatry. Because you have rejected the word of the LORD, He has also rejected you from being king" (1 Sam. 15:23). Did you catch that? Samuel was speaking under the anointing of God when he said rebellion is like the sin of divination.

What is divination? The Bible equates divination with witchcraft, fortune-telling, sorcery, idolatry, and other psychic phenomena, all of which were punishable by death in Old Testament times (Exod. 22:18; Deut. 13:12–15; 18:10). If spiritual rebellion is tantamount to divination, clearly this sort of attitude is much more than merely being an opinionated, strong-willed, or independent person. It is an attitude that sets itself up against God and His appointed representatives.

REBELLION CAN DESTROY YOU!

For example, when a child willfully disobeys his or her parents (assuming the parental instructions or commands are consistent with the Scriptures), the child is not only violating the fifth commandment—"Honor your father and your mother, that your days may be prolonged in the land which the LORD your God gives you" (Exod. 20:12)—but he or she is also rebelling against the parents' God-ordained authority, which is as serious an offense as practicing witchcraft!

When you rebel against your pastor, church board, or even a Sunday school teacher by harboring ill will in your heart or by speaking or acting in a disrespectful manner toward that person, watch out. God does not take such insubordination lightly.

Certainly those spiritual leaders in authority over you are only fallible human beings. Even the best leaders sometimes say or do things they shouldn't. Men and women who are sincerely dedicated to the Lord sometimes make unwise decisions or otherwise miss the mark. Nevertheless, even if you cannot respect the person, you should respect the office or position the person holds. The apostle Paul instructed us to "appreciate those who diligently labor among you, and have charge over you in the Lord and give you instruction, and that you esteem them very highly in love because of their work" (1 Thess. 5:12–13).

When you tolerate attitudes of hatred, bitterness, or resentment in your heart, you are opening the door of your life to demonic attack. It's like putting a big sign over your heart's door that says: "All you demons, come on in!" Demons love to live in a life filled with negative emotions. By harboring negative attitudes in your heart, you are offering them a safe haven. They don't have to seduce, deceive, or tempt you to make room for more demons. You are doing their dirty work for them.

Of course, once you open the door, the demons will come rushing in and will do their utmost to keep you bound by hatred, bitterness, or resentment. They will continually wrap more and more cords of animosity around your heart for as long as you allow them to do so.

Many Christians are living defeated lives even though they pray and read their Bibles, go to church, and give money to missions. Frequently the reason the devil has been able to wreak havoc in their lives is not because of their lack of commitment. It is because of their failure to forgive someone who hurt them in the past. Shelly was such a person.

Growing up, Shelly was a perky, attractive member of the National Honor Society in her school and an outspoken Christian who was unafraid to defend her faith. Her home life, however, was a different story. Shelly's mom and dad had divorced, so Shelly and her six-year-old brother, Stephen, lived in a small, shabby apartment with their mother.

Shelly's mom worked the three to eleven o'clock night shift as a waitress at the local truck stop, so Shelly spent most of her evenings studying, watching television, and babysitting Stephen. She rarely dated and was too ashamed to invite friends over to the apartment. Her only escape from her mundane existence was the time she spent with her church youth group every Sunday evening. There she met Jesus Christ.

Shelly studied the Bible and did her best to live a Christian life, but two problems kept coming back to haunt her. First, she missed her dad terribly, and second, she hated her mom for allowing the divorce to happen. Although Shelly knew the divorce had been mutual, she blamed her mom for causing her dad to leave. Shelly felt her mom had instigated the divorce, so it followed that it was also her mom's fault for the family's impoverished economic situation as well as Shelly's impoverished social life. Deep-seated bitterness and resentment continued to eat away at Shelly and created a constant tension between her and her mother.

It did something else too. It opened a door in Shelly's life to demonic attack. As a result Shelly became chronically depressed and remained so throughout her early adult years. Her attitude became increasingly lethargic, and she became physically sick. She frequently contemplated suicide.

Pastor Brian and some of Shelly's friends came to visit one evening. They had heard that Shelly had been sick and offered to pray for her. Pastor Brian asked Shelly if there were particular issues they should pray about. He wasn't prepared for

Shelly's response. She lashed out bitterly about her mom and dad's divorce and how her own life had been ruined as a result. "Everybody deserted me," she railed, "even God."

Pastor Brian recognized the root of bitterness that had grown up in Shelly's life. He said, "Shelly, I believe the Lord is leading me to tell you that you have never really let your mom and dad off the hook for getting divorced. You've never really forgiven them, and those roots of bitterness and resentment are wrapped around your heart. And if you don't repent and renounce them as the works of Satan that they are, they are going to kill you."

Shelly saw a seriousness in the pastor's face, and it scared her because she knew he was speaking the truth. She knelt down right there in front of her friends and repented for her rotten attitude. She asked God to forgive her and to cleanse her heart.

"Turn me upside down, Lord, and dump all the junk out of me," she prayed. "Then please turn my life right side up and fill me with You. And, Lord, please help me to love my parents, especially Mom, and help me to forgive them. Right now I want to take them off the hook for getting a divorce. I believe You have forgiven me of my sins, so I forgive Mom and Dad for theirs."

When Shelly got up from her knees, she looked as though a ten-ton weight had been lifted off her shoulders. For the first time in years she felt herself smiling then laughing and praising God along with her friends.

The next evening Shelly went to visit her mom. They had a heart-to-heart talk, and Shelly asked her mom to forgive her for her bad attitude. Then Shelly added, "And Mom, I want you to know that I forgive you and Dad for getting a divorce..."

Shelly had barely gotten the words out of her mouth when her mom burst into tears. She pulled Shelly close to her and hugged her tightly, weeping on her daughter's shoulder.

"Oh, Shelly, thank you!" her mom said through her tears. "I'm sure you've never understood all the details of your dad's and my divorce, and I've never really been able to talk about it very well with you. But all these years I've felt like a fish squirming on a hook. I couldn't get off, and the more I squirmed, the deeper the hook went into me. Now I finally feel like I've been taken off the hook."

Shelly stared back at her mother in amazement. She could hardly believe her ears. Her mom was describing their relationship in almost identical terms as Pastor Brian had done. Shelly told her mom about the pastor and her friends' visit, and specifically about the rebuke Pastor Brian had gently spoken to her. Then both Shelly and her mom had a good cry together. They spent most of the evening talking honestly and praying together and for each other. It was a new beginning for both of them.

If you have been harboring bitterness, resentment, pride, arrogance, unbelief, or any other negative attitude in your heart, please don't slough it off by saying, "Well, that's just me. That's part of my personality." Yes, that is you and your personality, but it is also sin, and it is giving the devil and his demons a wide-open shot at your heart. All of your efforts to stave off a frontal attack will be useless if you allow the "back door" of your life to remain open and unguarded. If you listen carefully, you can probably hear the sounds of the enemy hacking through the jungle.

Chapter Nine

WASH YOUR MOUTH
OUT WITH SOAP!

WHEN I WAS a little boy, if I said a curse word or spoke in some other evil fashion, my mom would take me upstairs to the bathroom sink, pick up a bar of soap, work up a good lather, and then make me wash my lips, tongue, and mouth. You can be sure I never said those words again…at least, not within Mom's earshot. Nowadays Mom would probably have been accused of child abuse, but I learned early on that words have a power of their own, and not all words are appropriate.

A lot of contemporary Christians could use a similar "mouth washing." Our mouths, which should be a medium of blessing people, are more frequently the means of cursing them. Of course, most of us never approach people and say, "I curse you," but by our negative comments and conversations we often allow our mouths to be weapons the devil can use to slice people to shreds. The wounds inflicted by words often hurt as much or more than physical blows. Many Christians have been devastated by negative statements spoken to or about them. Worse yet many of those searing words come out of the mouths of family members, friends, or fellow believers.

An important spiritual principle is at stake here. Author Dean Sherman says, "We can actually release supernatural blessing from our mouth, or we can aid the enemy's attack on people."[1]

James, one of the leaders in the early church after Christ's resurrection, wrote to the first-century Christians about this matter. You can almost see James shaking his head in frustration as he writes about the difficulty of taming the tongue and its power to do good or evil: "With it we bless our Lord and Father, and with it we curse men, who have been made in the likeness of God; from the same mouth come both blessing and cursing. My brethren, these things ought not to be this way" (James 3:9–10).

BLESSINGS AND CURSES ARE NO LAUGHING MATTER

Blessings and curses are taken seriously in the Bible. Entire chapters list the blessings that will come to God's people if they obey His Word and the curses that will come to those who don't (for example, see Deuteronomy 27–28). Noted Bible scholar T. Lewis, writing in the *International Standard Bible Encyclopedia*, explains:

> When a curse is pronounced against any person we are not to understand this as a mere wish, however violent, that disaster should overtake the person in question, any more than we are to understand that a corresponding "blessing" conveys simply a wish that prosperity should be the lot of the person on whom the blessing is invoked. A curse was considered to posses an inherent power of carrying itself into effect.[2]

In other words, this blessing and cursing stuff isn't hocus-pocus. Understand, when the Bible talks about cursing, it means much more than our modern ideas of swearing, uttering profanities, or using "dirty" words. To curse a person (according to the Old Testament) was to actually release spiritual power against him or her. That's why God said that He would curse anyone who cursed His people (Num. 24:9).

On the other hand, to bless someone also carried incredible significance. Once the words of blessing were spoken, the speaker could not retract them. Remember the story of Jacob and Esau? Jacob tricked their father, Isaac, into giving him the blessing that normally would have gone to the firstborn son, Esau (Gen. 27). The story would be foolish if the father's blessing wasn't worth having.

Many other instances of blessings are recorded in Scripture. Noah blessed his sons Shem and Japheth (Gen. 9:26–27); God blessed Abraham and told him that through Isaac, his son, he would become a great nation and a blessing to the entire world (Gen. 12:2–3, 22:17–18). Often the words of blessing were accompanied by the symbolic gesture of laying hands on the person who was to be blessed or lifting hands toward him or her. This is how Isaac may have blessed Jacob (Gen. 27:27–28) and Jacob, in turn, blessed his sons (Gen. 49:28). It is also how Jesus blessed His disciples (Luke 24:50) and the children who loved to gather around Him (Mark 10:16).

Jesus took the matter of blessings even further. Not only did He instruct us to bless one another and our families, but Jesus also instructed us to "bless those who curse you, pray for those who mistreat you" (Luke 6:28). The apostle Paul picked up the same point and expanded it: "Bless those who persecute you; bless and do not curse" (Rom. 12:14).

"What does all this have to do with spiritual warfare?", you may be wondering. Simply this: undoubtedly the devil and his demons understand the power of our words even better than we do. Whenever you spew forth a litany of negative, foul language, Satan and his assistants are right there, ready to ride the waves of those words as far as they can go, frequently right into a person's subconscious mind.

You desperately need to understand that your words are powerful, and your mouth can be either a means of blessing and encouragement or cursing and death. Scripture says, "Death and life are in the power of the tongue" (Prov. 18:21). Maybe that's why David prayed, "Set a guard, O LORD, over my mouth; keep watch over the door of my lips" (Ps. 141:3).

Our words have a life of their own. Once you have said them, whether they are positive or negative, they are out there. They never cease to exist.

Have you ever said something that you didn't really mean? Or perhaps the words came out of your mouth sounding much harsher than you intended? Quickly you say, "I take it back," but it is too late. Once spoken, it is impossible to retrieve our words.

That's why we need to be extremely careful about what we say about ourselves, about others, and about what we believe God wants us to do or what He wants to do in and through us. Let's look briefly at those three areas.

GUARD YOUR WORDS ABOUT YOURSELF

Ever since Adam and Eve first blew it in the Garden of Eden, human beings have been erring toward one extreme or the other regarding our opinions of ourselves. Sometimes we tend to think and speak more highly of ourselves than we should, leaning toward sinful pride. This attitude is rooted in an exalted view of self; it was the cause of the rebellion in the lives of Adam and Eve and resulted in their downfall and ultimate rejection from the garden.

On the other hand, we sometimes tend to wallow in the quagmire of low self-esteem. Because we know we are "fallen creatures," we think of ourselves as worthless and say simply awful things about ourselves. Many Christians confuse feeling sorry for themselves with true humility. They are obsessed with putting themselves down. Genuine humility is one of the grandest virtues a person can have. Unfortunately some people have substituted an attitude of self-belittling for the positive, holy trait of humility.

You know these sorts of people. They go around dragging themselves through the dirt, always putting themselves down by their words or actions. They live with the mistaken notion that they are being "lowly." "Be a doormat for Jesus!" is their motto, along with Rodney Dangerfield's famous remark, "I don't get no respect."[3] Such negative comments would be bad enough in themselves, but when Christians "spiritualize" their negative words and attitudes about themselves, thinking they are demonstrating how humble they are, their self-censure becomes an insult to God and an opportunity for Satan.

You've probably heard lines such as these before:

- "I guess God loves me, but I can't stand myself."
- "I'm good for nothing."
- "Everything I touch I mess up."
- "What a rotten person I am."
- "God could never use my life."

The truth is, these personal putdowns are not characteristic of genuine, Christlike humility. In fact, this sort of talk about ourselves runs counter to everything God has said about us. Christian humility means we are able to live without the incessant need to attract attention to ourselves. While we recognize our sinfulness, we refuse to dwell upon it, and when the Holy Spirit convicts us of sin, we are quick to repent of it. Rather than constantly talking about our shortcomings, we choose to concentrate on Christ and to center our conversations around Him—who He is, who we are in Him, and those things that are pleasing to Christ.

Honest humility acknowledges our strengths as well as our

weaknesses, our failures as well as our successes. We don't need to get puffed up over our successes, nor do we need to flagellate ourselves for our failures. In good times and bad, we can trust the Lord who has promised to use all things that come to us for His glory and for our good (Rom. 8:28).

Talking Dirty to Yourself

Knowing all this, why then do we continue to belittle ourselves? Stop and listen to some of the awful things you have been saying to and about yourself.

- "I'm such a jerk."
- "I can never do anything right."
- "If there is a way to mess up something, I'll find it."
- "I could never amount to anything for the Lord."
- "I can't stop smoking" (or drinking, or lying, or swearing, doing drugs, or living immorally).
- "I can't live the way God wants me to live."
- "I procrastinate all the time."
- "I can't get along with other people."
- "I hate myself."
- "I'm a poor student."

All the while, Satan is right there to "second" your motions and often adds to them. "That's right," he says. "You are a poor excuse for a human being. Nope, you could never do anything great for God. After all the horrible sins you have committed, how could you possibly think God could use somebody like *you*?" And where did the devil get all his ammunition? He got it from you by picking up on your own negative comments about yourself.

Imagine that you and your closest friend are walking down the street together when suddenly, for no reason at all, your buddy begins punching you in the stomach with all his might. Then, while you are doubled over in pain with the wind knocked out of you, he knees you in your nose. You fall to the ground, writhing in agony, and he begins to kick you and jump up and down all over you.

"Wait a minute!" I hear you shouting. "With friends like that…"

You are absolutely correct. Yet that is precisely what many people do to themselves. Through their negative words about themselves, they repeatedly beat up on themselves and then, masochistically, keep coming back for more! They harangue themselves with all sorts of despicable and demoralizing labels.

1. "What a klutz I am."

2. "You lamebrain."

3. "Way to go, moron."

4. "Dummy! Stupid! Motormouth! Worthless."

5. "Atta-boy, bonehead. What a nerd you are! You gross ogre. Fat slob."

6. "Loser!"

CHOOSE YOUR LABELS CAREFULLY

The labels you wear on your clothes aren't nearly as important as the labels you place upon yourself with your own words. The words you use to describe yourself will be manifested in the things you say and do.

I was explaining this principle to my nephew, Eric, on the golf course one day. Both of us were hitting the ball poorly, and Eric was becoming more frustrated and angry with every shot.

"Nice going, you moron!" he said to himself after a particularly bad shot.

"Eric, don't say that," I cautioned. "You are not a moron. You are intelligent, kind, sensitive, strong, generous, and an all-around decent guy. On top of all that, you're a pretty fine golfer."

"Yeah, well, thanks," Eric blushed self-consciously. "But what am I supposed to say when I hit a crummy shot?"

"Say, 'That sure wasn't like me. That was a poor shot, but the next one is going to be right where I want it.'"

We both took our next shots and promptly blasted two beautiful golf balls into oblivion, somewhere in the deep, dark "black hole" known only to golfers who are having bad days. Up and down the fairways, you could have heard, "That's not like me. That is *not* like me!"

"Me, neither!"

Guard your conversations about yourself because the devil and his demons are listening carefully, hoping to find a path through which they can penetrate your defenses.

GUARD YOUR WORDS ABOUT OTHERS

Have you ever noticed that Christians can say some terrible things about one another? Although we are reticent to admit it, most of us enjoy hearing something negative about another person, some juicy tidbit of hot gossip. Just listen to some of your conversations around the lunch table, at the gym, or wherever a group gathers—even those who congregate ostensibly in the Lord's name—and you will be shocked to discover how much of our talk centers around negative comments concerning other people, including gossip about fellow believers.

Satan loves it when Christians speak evil of one another. They are doing the devil's dirty work for him. No doubt, that is one reason why the apostle Paul had some firm words on this subject. The apostle said:

> Therefore, laying aside falsehood, SPEAK TRUTH EACH ONE OF YOU WITH HIS NEIGHBOR, for we are members of one another. BE ANGRY, AND YET DO NOT SIN; do not let the sun go down on your anger, and do not give the devil an opportunity....Let no unwholesome word proceed from your mouth, but only such a word as is good for edification according to the need of the moment, so that it will give grace to those who hear.
> —EPHESIANS 4:25–27; 29

Paul is basically saying, "Let's start building one another up with our words, rather than tearing one another down."

When it comes to un-Christlike talk, only one standard is acceptable: total abstinence. You can't play games with gossip; it will burn somebody every time. Even subtle slander, steeped in "Christianese," is out of bounds for a true believer. Have you ever tried to camouflage gossip with a prayer request? You know how it goes. "We really need to pray for Jody and Tim. I hear their marriage is in big trouble because Jody is fooling around with her boss." Of course, you rarely do pray for Jody and Tim. You just *talk* about praying for them, slandering their reputation as you pass on malicious morsels of gossip.

King David realized the danger of this subtle sin. He wrote, "Whoever secretly slanders his neighbor, him I will destroy" (Ps. 101:5). Jesus too reminded us of the eternal consequences of our words when He said, "Every careless word that people speak, they give an accounting for it in the day of judgment. For by your words you will be justified, and by your words you will be condemned" (Matt. 12:36–37).

Cautions like that should cause us to stop and think before

denigrating someone else. Make it a practice never to say any-thing behind the back of a brother or sister you have not already said to him or her face-to-face, or that you could not say while looking that person directly in the eyes. If you absolutely must comment about a person or situation, at least have the courage and the courtesy to preface your remark with a qualifier such as "In my opinion," or "It is my understanding," or "The way I see it." That way your reputation will be on the line as well.

Better still, attempt to be positive and Christlike in all your conversations about other people. Bless them with your words. If you can't bless them, at least don't curse them. Place an imagi-nary "Quiet, please" sticker over your lips. As the adage goes, "If you can't say anything good, then say nothing at all." Don't give the devil an opportunity to cause discord.

GUARD YOUR WORDS ABOUT GOD'S WORD

The devil loves to disrupt or divert the work of God through the negative words of God's own people. We need to understand that we can tear down in a moment with our mouths that which God has been planning, preparing, and molding His people to do for weeks, months, or even years.

We've all heard those infamous words that automatically spell death to new ideas within the body of Christ: "Well, we've never done it that way before..." Or, worse yet, "Yeah, well, we tried that once, and it didn't work."

Unfortunately almost every group of God's people is "blessed" with someone who can tell you all the reasons why you can't do what God has called you to do. A classic illustration of this took place when the people of God who had been delivered from the devil's bondage in Egypt came to borders of Canaan, God's dreamland for them. (See Numbers 13–14.) God had promised His people a rich possession, a land flowing with milk and honey, a fantastic future. There was only one problem: the Promised

Land that God had prepared for His people was already inhabited.

Anticipating a battle, Moses sent twelve spies into Canaan to check out the opposition. After six weeks the scouts came back with their report.

"It's just like we heard," they excitedly shared with the welcome party.

And all the people said, "Amen."

"It is a land flowing with milk and honey," the spies gushed. "Look at these grapes. Check out these pomegranates. Why, they're the biggest and best tasting we've ever seen. And here. Taste some of this honey. Isn't that something else?"

And all the people said, "Amen!"

But then came the bad news. "But there are giants in the land, and compared to them, we look like a bunch of grasshoppers."

And all the people said, "Oh, me; oh, my!"

"Therefore," concluded the spies, "we are not able to go in and take the land."

And all the people said, "We hear you, spies. Let's go back to Egypt."

All the people wanted to turn back, except two of the scouts, Joshua and Caleb, who said, "Whoa! Not so. We are well able to possess the land, *because our God has given it to us*."

Joshua and Caleb were not naïve or overly optimistic in their assessment. They had the same facts as their fellow spies. They admitted the existence of the giants, the opposition, and the obstacles, but the difference was *they believed God*. They refused to accept the words of their friends and family members whenever they contradicted the revealed Word of God. Furthermore they refused to see themselves as grasshoppers ready to be stomped upon by the enemy. Instead they saw themselves as

God's men, moving out as warriors according to God's Word to do God's will.

Joshua and Caleb had the same data as the doubters and those who insisted upon speaking and hearing about the negative reports, but they drew different conclusions. Consequently, of more than two million people who came out of Egypt, only *two*, Joshua and Caleb, eventually entered God's Promised Land. The others were a reproach to God's name. They dishonored Him with their mouths (as well as with their minds and hearts), and as a result spent the rest of their lives wandering around in circles throughout the wilderness until they died. God raised up an entirely new generation of warriors who were willing to trust His Word, and they went in and conquered the land.

I believe God is doing something similar today. That's why it is vital that we guard our minds and hearts and carefully watch our words, not giving the devil an opportunity to launch a successful sneak attack or any other sort of subterfuge.

The group of warriors who grew up in the wilderness had to learn the lessons of their fathers and mothers, both the good and the bad. More than that they had to learn who and where the enemy was. But because they had never known anything but dry, dirty, uncomfortable, wandering wilderness living, they were excited about driving out the enemy and getting in on the promises of God.

That's where I see the current crop of wilderness warriors in God's kingdom. They are ready to fight for what God has said belongs to them. Come on; hold onto your hat. We're getting ready to step into enemy territory.

Chapter Ten

THE WRESTLER AND THE WARRIOR

BEFORE YOU ENTER the fracas, it is important to understand the various types of opponents we are fighting. In Ephesians 6:10–18 the apostle Paul gives us two illustrations describing our engagement with the enemy: the wrestler and the warrior. First Paul warns us: "For our struggle is not against flesh and blood, but against the rulers, against the powers, against the world forces of this darkness, against the spiritual forces of wickedness in the heavenly places" (v. 12).

When you first read Paul's words, it sounds as though he is just on a spiritual roll, but that is not the case. Every word is chock-full of meaning.

In the King James Version of the Bible, the word "struggle" is translated "wrestle." In Paul's day wrestling was a much more prominent sport than it is today. It was extremely popular among spectators, who cheered on their favorite athletes. There was, however, one main difference between the wrestling matches of old and those of our day. The loser frequently lost more than the match; the loser in a Greek wrestling match had his eyes gouged out!

Unlike some sports, wrestling requires a great deal of physical contact with the opponent. But it takes more than sheer might and power to win a wrestling match. A good wrestler knows that to come out on top, he must outthink his opponent.

Consequently wrestling requires an incredible amount of concentration and constant exertion of energy. To let up, even for a moment, is to give your opponent the advantage.

Looks can be deceiving during a wrestling match. Sometimes you may see two wrestlers locked motionless in a hold or grip, and by all outward appearances it looks as though they are loafing. People unfamiliar with the sport or who have never engaged in a wrestling match themselves might say, "Look at those guys. They're kneeling there, holding onto each other and not doing anything significant. You call this exciting?"

What the uninitiated wrestling fan fails to understand is that even in those times of apparent inactivity, the wrestlers are expending huge amounts of physical energy in their efforts to overcome each other. If you could use a stress meter to measure the pressure they are placing upon each other's bodies, the needle on the meter would be slamming into the red danger zone.

The wrestlers cannot call time-out or take a break. The match goes on until one of the wrestlers is pinned to the floor or the allotted time for the match expires. It is truly a fight to the finish.

Similar to wrestling, there are no time-outs in spiritual warfare; the battle goes on day and night. The devil doesn't take vacations, nor does he celebrate holidays by taking a day or two off work. That's why the apostle Peter said, "Be of sober spirit, be on the alert. Your adversary, the devil, prowls around like a roaring lion, seeking someone to devour. But resist him, firm in your faith" (1 Pet. 5:8–9).

This lion never sleeps. He creeps around constantly, looking for someone to attack. You needn't let that frighten you, but you should always be aware of the potential danger.

In one of the neighborhoods where we lived years ago, the neighbors across the street owned a beautiful white Labrador they named "Buckwheat." He was a friendly dog, but he was huge. One day I heard our car horn blowing incessantly in our driveway. I went outside and saw that Buckwheat was standing upright with his back paws on the ground and his front paws on the car's roof above the door. My wife and children were so frightened they didn't want to get out of the car. I couldn't really blame them; it took my full strength to pull Buckwheat off the vehicle.

Ordinarily our neighbors kept Buckwheat in a pen or on a leash, but occasionally they let him run loose. When Buckwheat got a glimpse of our young daughters playing in our back-yard, the dog bolted across the street, raced into our yard, and knocked the girls off their feet. He never bit the girls, but he sure gave us all a few scares. We taught our girls that when-ever they saw Buckwheat approaching, they were to call out to Daddy and immediately climb higher into their tree house until Daddy could get there to deal with Buckwheat.

Was our family aware of Buckwheat? Oh, yes. Were we afraid of him? Not really. Our girls learned that Daddy was stronger than the dog, and when the hound came howling onto our prop-erty, all they had to do was to call out to Daddy, and help would be on the way.

My family's attitude toward Buckwheat is similar to the way we regard the devil. Are we aware of him? Oh, yes. Are we afraid of him? Absolutely not. We know whenever he comes lurking around our lives, all we need to do is to call out to our heavenly Father.

Some Bible teachers explain Peter's illustration of the devil as a roaring lion (1 Pet. 5:8) by saying Satan is a lion on a long leash. The devil, they say, cannot touch you; he can only go so far before the leash yanks him back into place. If, however, you step into his sphere of influence, the roaring lion can reach you, and he will rip you apart.

I like that illustration but would add one thing. I think the leash is similar to the "remote control" leash our neighbors purchased for Buckwheat. The dog was fitted with a special collar with a battery-operated receiver built into it. His masters owned the remote control along with the transmitter. Since Buckwheat was not tied down by any visible leash, to most people it looked as though he was a free agent.

He was free to roam around our neighbors' land as far as he wanted to run, but the moment the neighbors saw him step over the line, they pressed a button on the transmitter that sent a high-frequency signal to Buckwheat's collar. Buckwheat quickly learned through experience that the signal meant STOP WHERE YOU ARE, RIGHT NOW. Although we could not see the button being pressed or hear the high-frequency signal, we could see the results of this invisible encounter. Buckwheat always went back home sulking.

Something similar happens in the spirit realm whenever the devil or his demons try to attack you. If you are living with clean hands and a pure heart and not stepping inside the devil's sphere of influence by opening the door to sin, the devil cannot touch you. When the lion attempts to leap across those boundaries, the "heavenly transmitter" sounds, and God dispatches His angels to pull the demons off your case.

That is not to imply that bad things do not sometimes happen to good people, or that by committing isolated acts of sin you are negating the God's power or willingness to protect you. We are in a war, after all, and as in any conflict, even good soldiers, as well as innocent people, can make mistakes, stumble, fall, or otherwise get hurt. But by keeping your heart pure and staying close to Jesus, you have nothing to fear.

You Can't Tell the Players Without a Scorecard

Going back to Paul's picture of he wrestler (Eph. 6:12), notice that the apostle doesn't suggest that we wrestle directly against the devil. Partly this is because Satan can be only in one place at a time, and he normally has more important business to attend to than you or me. Paul does instruct us, though, that we can expect to encounter the demonic hordes to whom Satan has delegated evil responsibilities. Paul names several categories of demonic opposition we are likely to engage: rulers, powers and authorities, rulers of darkness, and spiritual forces of wickedness in the heavenly places. Most Bible scholars believe these categories represent various areas of demonic influence in our world.

Rulers

The word the apostle Paul uses to describe these demonic rulers is *archai*, which reminds us of the term "archangel." The word can also be translated as "principalities" or "princes."[1] An example of these high-level satanic princes can be found in Daniel 10:13, 20, where the satanic angel known as the prince of Persia tried to block the heavenly angel assigned by God to bring the answer of Daniel's prayers. The battle took place in the invisible realm of the heavenlies for twenty-one days before the heavenly archangel, Michael, came to help defeat the prince of Persia and his chief princes (Dan. 10:12–13). Daniel also mentions an upcoming battle with the prince of Greece (v. 20).

In his book *The Adversary* Mark Bubeck sees these devilish archangels as having enormous power and a tremendous amount of freedom to operate under Satan's auspices.[2] Similarly author and former Fuller Theological Seminary professor Dr. C. Peter Wagner regards this type of demonic angel as a "territorial spirit," a satanic archangel that has "rulership" over a particular area.[3] That rulership may be over a city, state, or nation, but possibly it may be over an area of influence such as education, arts, and entertainment, or the world political systems.

Powers and authorities

The word "powers" is used in Ephesians 6:12 in the King James Version and comes from the Greek word *dunamis*. The word used in this verse, however, is *exousia*. The New International Version correctly translates *exousia* as "authorities" or "strongholds." These may be demons that attempt to influence the governments and authority structures of our world. These powers and authorities also seem to specialize in various kinds of sin, perhaps concentrating on an attempt to subvert people through a particular sin such as homosexuality, murder, greed, or others.

Don't misunderstand; these powers cannot force a person to indulge in sinful lifestyles, but if individuals in a particular city or nation condone or give themselves over to certain types of sin, the demonic powers will establish a stronghold there. Sodom and Gomorrah are examples of this, two cities that established themselves as centers of moral corruption; their very names are associated with vice, depravity, and homosexuality (Gen. 19:1–11).

Something similar is happening in our day. Certain cities are known as havens for pornography; others have established a reputation for their openness to occult activities, homosexuality, mindless murders, gambling, or misuse of money. Sadly these sins are committed in nearly every location nowadays, but some cities and towns "not only do the same, but also give hearty approval to those who practice them" (Rom. 1:32).

Rulers of darkness

These "world forces of darkness" are apparently lower on the devil's "totem pole," and most Bible scholars believe these rulers and their underlings are the types of demons you and I are probably going to encounter most frequently. It could be that these rulers of darkness are sort of the "foremen" overseeing the fourth category of demons in hell's hierarchy.

Forces of wickedness

These wicked, evil spiritual forces operate in the "heaven-lies," not simply in the clouds, but in the spiritual realm that surrounds us. Sometimes these demons take on names for themselves that coincide with the point of entry they find into a person's life, such as "lust," "greed," or "suicide." Sometimes demons assume false labels, such as "healer" or "paralyzer." All of these demons are lying spirits; they will lie to you and about you.

Reverend David Manske, a member of a missionary team working in Brazil, encountered these kinds of evil spirits in a man named Sergio. Sergio's wife had called the missionaries, begging for someone who could help her husband. Sergio agreed to come to the church to meet with David and Steve Renicks, another missionary.

When Sergio and his wife arrived at the church, the missionaries began by asking the man some simple questions. Almost immediately the demons within Sergio began manifesting themselves. Sergio started screaming and thrashing about on the floor and attempted to strike the missionaries with his fists. But the power of Jesus Christ in the men of God was greater than the power of the demons. As much as Sergio tried to hit or grab Steve or David, he was unable to do so. His hands never touched the missionaries.

Nevertheless for the next three hours the missionaries battled the demons. Rev. Manske described the encounter:

> The spirits, speaking through Sergio, gave wrong information, accused Sergio's wife, complained about the "weight" of our Christian hands, challenged our authority and repeatedly stated that they were in charge of Sergio's

life. One of the spirits displayed a genuine hatred for God's Word. Under this spirit's control Sergio bit at the Bible, chomping deep into the cover, and shredding its pages with a jerk of his head....During the encounter a complaining spirit whimpered about physical pain, while another spoke of suicide and killing Sergio.[4]

As David and Steve continued to work with Sergio to defeat the demons in him, Sergio's wife explained how the demonic attacks had started. The previous New Year's Eve Sergio, dressed in black and with bottles of wine dedicated to Satan, had made a pact with the devil. Although Sergio's wife wasn't sure of the details, she knew that in return for certain "favors," the devil had demanded Sergio's life before midnight on the day of Sergio's thirty-first birthday. The evening Sergio and his wife came to the church for help was his birthday—his thirty-first birthday.

As midnight approached, the demons within Sergio fought harder for his life, but Steve and David continued praying for him, singing praises to God and reading Psalm 34 and other Scripture passages to Sergio. The turning point came, however, when Sergio himself began reading the Scripture aloud. The demons attempted to distort Sergio's mind, causing him to make errors as he read the Scripture, but the missionaries confronted the evil spirits by the power and authority of Jesus Christ, and Sergio continued to read. Finally, after more than three hours of wrestling, the demons gave up. It was shortly after midnight when Sergio was set free.

Most Christians will probably never be called upon to become involved in casting out demons, but you should definitely be aware that these situations occur and are not the results of over-active imaginations. On the other hand, many Christians will encounter "combat situations" with evil spirits and rulers of world forces that operate through witchcraft, Satanism, fortune-tellers, psychics, mediums, and other occult practices. Other

Christians may find it necessary to engage in conflicts with territorial spirits who are holding sway over an entire area.

Whatever level of battle in which you find yourself, in any direct confrontations with the enemy you should always work together with teams of Christians if at all possible. When it comes to spiritual warfare, although one Christian who is under the control of the Holy Spirit is enough to defeat the enemy by using the authority of Jesus's name, a group of mature believers adds strength and wisdom.

THE WARRIOR

After establishing that spiritual warfare is similar to a wrestling match, Paul paints another graphic word-picture in Ephesians 6:10–18, using a Roman soldier to describe our battle. Paul instructs us to "put on the full armor of God, so that you will be able to stand firm against the schemes of the devil" (v. 11). The apostle's original readers well understood this illustration, since Rome's soldiers kept the peace throughout the Empire with an iron fist and were visible to most people any day of the week. Paul's readers knew the weaponry of Roman soldiers.

Paul picked up on an important point: namely, that the Roman soldiers' armor protected the front of the soldier but not the back. This wasn't an oversight by an Italian uniform designer. It was done on the purposeful assumption that a Roman soldier would be moving toward his enemy, not running away. Furthermore the uniform and weapons made a silent statement that a Roman soldier's first responsibility was not to protect himself but to move forward and defeat the enemy. To Paul it made perfect sense that a Christian "soldier" engaging in spiritual warfare should adopt that same attitude. You won't win many battles in spiritual warfare if you turn your back to the enemy.

Paul also noted that although the evil one, the devil, launches flaming missiles (v. 16) from a distance, the Christian's primary offensive weapon is "the sword of the Spirit, which is the word of God" (v. 17). Paul's implication is obvious: for the Christian, spiritual warfare takes place up close. No wonder Paul spent so much time explaining how to dress for the conflict. Let's take a look at what Paul would have considered "dressing for success."

Chapter Eleven

YOUR WARDROBE AND
YOUR WEAPONS

I HAVE TO CONFESS. As a young Christian I absolutely *hated* to hear sermons or read books about the armor of God. To me it smacked of knights in shining armor, Sir Lancelot, Guinevere, and King Arthur: cute, but certainly not relevant to me as a new Christian struggling to put my newfound faith into practice. Whenever my pastor waxed eloquent about the necessity of putting on the full armor of God, I'd stare back at him with a disdainful scowl on my face as if to say, "Why don't you talk about something important?" Little did I know that the man was trying to save my life!

Learning how to put on the full armor of God is imperative. But talking or reading about it isn't enough. Beyond learning about the armor of God, we need to do what God says and start using it. Let me ask you a straightforward question. Do you put on the full armor of God every day? If you are like most Christians (and if you answer honestly), you will probably say, "No, not really."

Why not? Lack of knowledge? Laziness? Overconfidence? Whatever your excuse, forget it and make it a habit to "suit up" every day. Can you imagine a football player going out to play without wearing any pads and dressed only in his underwear? Oh, sure; the player might stay in the game for a few plays, as long as he didn't get hit. But without the proper protection football can be a dangerous game.

We've already seen that spiritual warfare is much more serious than a football game. How much more then do we need to put on the right outfit if we hope to succeed in defeating the enemy?

Why Should I Put on Armor?

The apostle Paul gives us two simple reasons we need to put on the armor of God. First, in Ephesians 6:11, he writes: "Put on the full armor of God, so that you will be able to stand firm against the schemes of the devil."

If you turn Paul's statement around, it is clear that if you do not put on the whole armor of God, you won't be able to stand against the deceptive schemes of Satan. We've already established that the devil doesn't fight fairly but delights in pulling dirty tricks on you. How are you going to stand against that stuff if you are unprotected?

The second reason Paul tells us to put on the full armor of God is in verse 13: "Therefore, take up the full armor of God, so that you will be able to resist in the evil day, and having done everything, to stand firm." Notice, you are to put on the *full* armor of God. It will do you little good to put on only a portion of your protection. Satan has an uncanny ability to find and play upon your weaknesses. If you are unprotected in a particular area, the devil will attempt to exploit you in that vulnerable place.

Again the reverse of Paul's statement is also true: if you do not put on the full armor, you will not be able to resist the devil in the evil day. What evil day is Paul talking about? Certainly he is alluding to the evil days that are to come at the end of the world as we know it, but Paul also could be talking about today, tomorrow, or any day the demonic forces attack you. Without proper protection, the devil will overwhelm you in a moment. But with the armor of God you can stand against anything Satan throws at you.

OUR WEAPONS ARE MORE THAN DEFENSIVE

For years most pastors and teachers I heard speak on the subject of the armor of God emphasized that our weapons are all defensive except for the sword of the Spirit, the Word of God. These teachings made it sound as though Christians should never go on the offensive and attack Satan's strongholds. They implied that our job was to stand firm and to keep ducking the devil's fiery darts or deflecting them with our shields of faith, all the while hoping that we didn't get overwhelmed.

Frankly, to me, the whole idea of "standing firm," as I heard it presented, sounded repulsive. It conjured up images in my mind of a bunch of Christians hiding out behind the church organ, saying, "Shhh. If we stay quiet, maybe nobody will know we are here!"

As I began studying the Scripture more closely, however, I discovered that "standing firm" doesn't mean you are to simply stand there and let the devil beat up on you. It refers more to the triumphant stance of a victorious army that, having devastated the domains of the enemy, can stand its ground with confidence. Of course, you can never do that under your own strength; that is Paul's primary point about spiritual warfare: "Finally, be strong in the Lord and in the strength of His might" (Eph. 6:10).

Notice it is the Lord's strength we are relying upon as we engage the enemy, not our own. And what incredible strength it is! The "strength of His might" is the phrase Paul uses in Ephesians 1:19–20 to describe the supernatural power "which He brought about in Christ, when He raised Him from the dead and seated Him at His right hand in the heavenly places."

In other words, the same divine power that defeated the devil when Jesus rose from the dead is available to you now to defeat any diabolical plot hatched in hell against you.

Paul's balanced formula for success in spiritual warfare is simple: we can be confident in the Lord's strength, but we need to daily put on the full armor of God if we want to stand firm against the schemes of the devil. The apostle reminds us that we are not fighting a political system, the church across town, some other human institution, or even another religion. We are warring against a powerful, complex array of supernatural entities that have thoroughly infiltrated the "air space" around us and are exerting awful influences over the world systems with which we live.

But to imply that God's people are simply to sit back and allow Satan and his demons to blast away at us is an erroneous assumption. A warrior who only defends himself and never takes steps to disarm and drive out the enemy will soon be fighting the same battle again. A Christian who does not get involved in the war is defeated already.

Furthermore, to say that our weapons are mostly defensive is like the Pentagon saying the same thing about the United States' armed forces. Certainly our military might has been a strong deterrent against attacks upon our country and others by enemy forces. But as we have seen in history, the United States military can also be awesome when used for offensive purposes.

The Roman shield, helmet, breastplate, and girdle were likewise both defensive and offensive. When the Roman soldiers took up their armor, they advanced together in what history records as the invincible Roman wedge. Their shields were not round but oblong, or rectangular, as much as four feet in length and two and a half feet wide. Each soldier covered his own body with two-thirds of his shield while using one-third of his shield to help cover his buddy on his left. When the Roman soldiers tightened their ranks, the unit formed an awesome wedge of shields moving together across the battlefield.

As Paul wrote about our spiritual wardrobe and weapons, he probably had that powerful wedge in mind, thinking of the church as a group of soldiers standing shoulder to shoulder, each person partly responsible for the person next to him or her as we move into enemy territory. Paul did not depict our spiritual wardrobe and weaponry in this manner for no purpose; on the contrary, the apostle expects the church to win its battles, not merely to avoid getting beaten up. Everything about our warrior's wardrobe and weaponry speaks of victory, not simply survival.

THE GIRDLE OF TRUTH

The sound of the word *girdle* nearly gagged me when I first read this passage. To me a girdle was something somebody wore to help contain his or her fat. It didn't sound like part of a soldier's uniform.

Actually the phrase "HAVING GIRDED YOUR LOINS WITH TRUTH" (Eph. 6:14) indicates a readiness for action. Today we might say, "Roll up your sleeves," or "Roll up your pant legs." The tougher question is, what is the "truth" to which Paul is referring?

Nowadays few people want to talk in terms of absolute truth. Everything is "relative." Ironically on many university campuses the one statement that will get a student into trouble faster than any other is, "I know so." Those students who are "foolish" enough to believe that there are absolute standards of right and wrong run the risk of being ridiculed, ostracized, or possibly flunked, especially if their ideas about truth reflect a biblical base.

The apostle Paul met a group of pseudo-intellectual "scholars" in Acts 17:17–18. He was talking with some Jews and some

God-fearing Gentiles, but most of his listeners were pagan philosophers who didn't know the first thing about Jesus Christ. These Greek, Epicurean, and Stoic philosophers—guys with names such as Plato, Aristotle, Socrates, Euripides, Sugar-diabetes, and Mercedes—spent most of their time sitting around dressed in their long flowing robes, stroking their beards, and looking for and debating what new thing might be true.

"Mercedes, what do you think is true?"

"I don't know, Diabetes. What do you think is true?"

"No fair, I asked you first. What about you, Euripides? What do you think is true?"

"Well, I'm not absolutely sure, but I think something may be true today that wasn't true yesterday, but then again I'm not sure if it will be true tomorrow..." (Images of the buzzards in *Jungle Book* come to mind.)

Interesting, isn't it? When you don't really know what is true, you are willing to accept almost any new idea in the name of tolerance, regardless of how outlandish it may be. Unfortunately that is precisely where much of our society is today, and as a result Satan is having a heyday.

Jesus said, "I am the way, and the truth, and the life; no one comes to the Father but through Me" (John 14:6). To gird your loins with His truth means to wrap yourself up in His Word, especially the truth of the gospel. The Bible is your standard for truth. The devil, remember, attempts to distort that truth or otherwise get you to doubt God's Word. Don't do it. Jesus said, "You will know the truth, and the truth will make you free" (John 8:32).

THE BREASTPLATE OF RIGHTEOUSNESS

This sounds like something out of a Conan the Barbarian movie, but actually it is a quotation from Isaiah 59:17: "He put on righteousness like a breastplate, and a helmet of salvation on His head." This is a prophetic word about Jesus. If Jesus needed to put on the armor of God to live His life in obedience to His heavenly Father and in victory over Satan, how much more do you and I need to put on this armor?

Roman soldiers wore breastplates to protect their hearts from enemy blows. The best modern counterpart to the ancient breastplate is a bulletproof vest used by police or military personnel. The wearer may take a shot to the body, but the vest will protect him or her from lethal blows to the heart. Similarly Paul says the best spiritual protection for your heart is right living before God. If you are living with a clean heart, though the strongest demons may attack, they cannot ultimately hurt you.

PUT ON YOUR "GOSPEL SHOES"

In Ephesians 6:15 Paul tells us to put on some good running shoes, "with your feet fitted with the readiness that comes from the gospel of peace" (NIV). Paul's point is that we should be ready to take the gospel of Jesus Christ to anybody, anywhere, anytime. Readiness is the overriding theme of Paul's teaching on spiritual warfare. This readiness includes not only a willingness to share the gospel with others but also a preparation to fight for the right to be heard above the noise of the demonic din.

Footwear manufacturer LA Gear once sold an athletic shoe with a battery-powered light in the heel that allowed the wearer's shoes to be seen moving in the darkness. The Christian has "Holy Spirit–powered" shoes that can also be seen taking the gospel into the darkest parts of the world. Your responsibility is to put on these shoes daily and then be ready to take His gospel of peace wherever the Lord directs you.

At times you may be tempted to think, "I don't want to go to that place, Lord. I'm not sure I am ready for this." Jesus then says something like, "That's OK. I am ready to go there. You just put on My shoes, and let's get moving." When the Spirit of Christ is walking with you and through you, He will give you the courage and the strength to take the next step of obedience to His will.

THE SHIELD OF FAITH

Next, Paul says you are to take up "the shield of faith with which you will be able to extinguish all the flaming arrows of the evil one" (v. 16). In Paul's day the shield was one of the most important pieces of equipment the soldier could carry. The shield was the soldier's primary weapon against the flaming arrows, or "fiery darts," to which Paul refers. These flaming darts were basically arrows soaked in pitch, then set on fire and launched. The fiery darts were effective even if they did not score a direct hit on the soldier, simply because of the fear and confusion their fierce blazes caused. If you can imagine the effects of a firebomb in our day, you will have the idea.

The large Roman shield was an excellent weapon with which to stave off these attacks of the enemy. Sometimes the fire arrows simply bounced off the shield. At other times the fiery darts sank into the shield's surface and burned out by themselves.

The devil is still hurling fiery darts today. Satan's fiery arrows may take the form of temptation; lies (especially lies set ablaze by a fiery tongue bearing gossip, which divides the church's troops); insults; sarcastic remarks; personal setbacks; false teaching; persecutions; impure thoughts, attitudes, or conduct; and probably many more. Nevertheless, none of these fiery darts of the devil can penetrate our shield of faith. It is our faith in Jesus Christ that causes us to stand, not faith in our own abilities, personalities, or gifts. He is our shield, and He protects us.

THE HELMET OF SALVATION

When I played high school football, every once in a while some of us guys would get in a silly mood and put our helmets on backward. Then we'd try to tackle one another. Besides not fitting well, the backward helmets blocked our vision. We usually played this game near the biggest mud hole we could find on the practice field, so you can guess where most everybody landed.

It was always a hilarious scene—players lunging foolishly at each other, trying to make contact with the opposition but missing completely and landing in the mud. Even if a player happened to hit another, it was such a surprise the jolt usually sent the attacker reeling as well as the person impacted by the blow. Football helmets are meant to be worn facing forward.

In a similar manner, the helmet of salvation (v. 17) works best when we wear it face-forward, not looking backward to past failures (or even past victories), but looking ahead toward the territories yet to be conquered.

Your head, of course, is one of the most vulnerable areas on your body. No wonder the devil works overtime attacking you with evil thoughts, vile imaginations, and impure daydreams. Then, through nasty nightmares, Satan tempts us toward fear or doubt. Again this is why it is so important that "we demolish arguments and every pretension that sets itself up against the knowledge of God, and we take captive every thought to make it obedient to Christ" (2 Cor. 10:5, NIV).

The Bible says that as Christians "we have the mind of Christ" (1 Cor. 2:16). Practically this means if a thought would not be appropriate for Jesus, you and I should reject it too. When you find yourself drifting toward evil thoughts, ask yourself, "Would Jesus dwell on this idea?" We need to guard our mental input every day, casting out any thought that is displeasing to, or unlike, Jesus Christ.

The best way to do that is to put on "the helmet of salvation." Defensively the helmet protects our minds from doubts and impurities; offensively it gives us confidence to know that we can aggressively attack the enemy without fear of "losing our salvation" or falling into sin. But always remember, the helmet is useless to you unless you put it on each day.

THE SWORD OF THE SPIRIT

The sword of the Spirit is the Word of God (Eph. 6:17). It is not meant to be used merely as a defensive weapon but also as an offensive weapon against the devil and his demons. Notice too that it is the Holy Spirit who gives this sword its "cutting edge." Have you ever heard a person read or quote scripture but it seems to lack any real power? It is not because the Word of God itself is powerless, but because the person spouting scripture is merely mouthing words without the anointing power of the Holy Spirit.

Satan knows the power of this sword, so he does all he can to keep the Word of God from being presented. For instance, once Corrie ten Boom, the saintly woman of God who survived the Nazi concentration camps, was speaking at a conference of Bible students in Japan. Corrie spoke through an interpreter, but the young woman assigned to translate could not understand Corrie's illustrations. Corrie tried other ways to present the scriptural truth she wanted to impart to the students, but the interpreter still couldn't grasp the meaning. Finally, in frustration, the young translator burst into tears.

Corrie began to think: "For what reason am I unable to bring God's message to them? Here is the devil at work." The first step on the way to victory is to recognize the enemy. The devil is a conquered enemy, and we have the privilege and the authority to fight him in the name of the Lord Jesus.

Corrie paused in her attempts to present her message to the

students and spoke directly to the translator: "Dark power that hinders this girl from interpreting God's message—I command you in the name of the Lord Jesus to leave her alone. She is meant to be a temple of the Holy Spirit, not your temple." The girl immediately began to interpret Corrie's message fluently, and the meeting was greatly blessed.[1]

Whenever you find yourself under demonic attack, ask the Holy Spirit to empower your mind and mouth, and then begin quoting Scripture to Satan. He hates it. Have you ever seen a vampire movie? (I'm not recommending that you do.) The hero flashes a cross in the face of the vampire, and the fiendish ghoul cringes at the sight. Obviously vampires are fictional, and we know the cross is only a symbol with no power of its own, except that it represents the death and resurrection of our Lord Jesus. Nevertheless, something like the vampire's response really does happen whenever a Spirit-filled believer begins quoting the Bible to the devil. The Word of God is the sword of the Spirit, and Satan learned long ago that he is powerless against it.

HOW TO PUT ON THE ARMOR

Did you happen to notice how much the armor of God sounds like characteristics of Jesus? He is the truth. He is our righteousness. He is our peace; our faith is in Him. He is our salvation, and He is the Word: "In the beginning was the Word, and the Word was with God, and the Word was God" (John 1:1). In a real sense, then, when we put on the whole armor of God, we are "putting on Jesus." When you are a Christian, He is already in you (1 John 4:4; Col. 1:27), but when you put on the armor of God, you are taking on Christlike characteristics externally as well. You may look the same or feel the same about yourself (probably better because of the confidence Christ gives you), but in a real way your life becomes a reflection of Jesus.

After a while putting on the armor of God becomes a habit,

a natural part of preparing to meet each new day, like brushing your teeth or slipping into your favorite pair of shoes. You hardly have to think about it; you just do it. Until taking up the armor becomes part of your routine, this spiritual exercise will help you get started.

As soon as you are semiconscious each morning, before you go out to meet the day, stop; look in the mirror, and say, "Jesus, You are my armor. I believe in You, and I know You are alive in me. Now, by an act of my will, I put on the armor of God. You are the truth, and I gird myself with the truth right now. Please be the truth in my life today." Do something similar for each piece of armor.

1. Gird your loins in truth.

2. Put on the breastplate of righteousness.

3. Put on your "gospel shoes."

4. Take up the shield of faith.

5. Put on the helmet of salvation.

6. Pick up the sword of the Spirit, the Word of God. (While you are at it, you may as well take a few minutes to read the Word.)

Make your prayer personal, present tense, and active as you claim each piece of God's armor. In other words, rather than saying, "Lord, please give me the shield of faith," pray aloud, "Lord, I take up the shield of faith."

PRAYER IS THE KEY

As Paul sums up what our wardrobe should be, he emphasizes our primary weapon in spiritual warfare: prayer. The apostle writes: "With all prayer and petition pray at all times in the Spirit, and with this in view, be on the alert with all perseverance and petition for all the saints" (Eph. 6:18). Prayer is the key to all effective spiritual warfare. For your own sake and for the safety of others who live and work with you, if prayer is not a priority in your life, please stay as far away from the front lines of spiritual warfare as possible. You might get seriously hurt, and at the risk of sounding like an extremist, you could get killed.

Spiritual warfare is not fun and games or Halloween high jinks. Satan and the demons under his control are more warped and wicked than any person you have ever met. Their hearts and minds are evil beyond measure, and every intent of their being is malevolent and malicious. They are much more powerful than mere human beings who, without prayer, are operating in their own wisdom and human energy. Many Christians who have regarded spiritual warfare as just another spiritual jag, sort of the latest "spiritual rush," have been severely injured physically, emotionally, and spiritually.

On the other hand, if you will put on the full armor of God every day and use the spiritual weapons the Lord has provided, you can engage the enemy with confidence, defeat him in the name of Jesus, and come away with a Christ-honoring testimony. But as with any weapon, to be effective you must know how to use them. That's what we need to look at next.

Chapter Twelve

GUNS AND ROSES

I HAVE NEVER OWNED a gun in my life. The closest I came to gun ownership took place during my first year in college when I enrolled in Reserve Officers' Training Corps (ROTC). As part of my training I received an M-1 rifle for which I was responsible. I carried that gun with pride. I studied that gun. I learned how to take it apart piece by piece, how to clean each part, and how to put it all back together again. I learned how to "present arms" with my gun. I carried it on my shoulder as my platoon marched up and down the football field, practicing our drills. I carried it in parades. The one thing I never did with my gun was shoot it.

A lot of Christians are like that when it comes to spiritual warfare. They study the subject; they listen carefully to sermons about it; they read books about it—they just never get around to doing it. In this chapter you will discover some of the spiritual arsenal at your disposal. However, all of this information will never drive the devil out of your life unless you put these weapons to use.

YOUR WEAPONS ARE SPIRITUAL

Although it might be obvious to many Christians, we need constant reminders that our weapons are spiritual, not physical. Remember Paul's words: "For though we walk in the flesh, we do not war according to the flesh, for the weapons of our warfare

are not of the flesh, but divinely powerful for the destruction of fortresses" (2 Cor. 10:3–4). Most of us are so accustomed to taking things into our own hands, trying to solve things "our way," we frequently forget that our way is not necessarily "God's way." Furthermore, with so many awful problems facing us as individuals and as a society, it is easy to get caught up trying to change the world through physical action while forgetting that the underlying problems are spiritual in nature.

Even in churches, much of the problem solving is done with fleshly, worldly methods resulting in fleshly, worldly solutions. In many churches serving in a leadership position can be hazardous to your health, literally. People will yell at you, scream at you, and threaten you. They will insult you and attempt to undermine your reputation. Who needs that? In one church during an open congregational meeting members tore into their church leaders and one another, trading insults back and forth across the crowded room. The leaders responded in kind, and at several points the church meeting threatened to turn into a prizefight.

All supposedly in the name of Jesus.

Arguments, manipulations, backbiting, church cliques and dictatorships, family feuds—are these the church's weapons of warfare? Absolutely not! These are tools of the devil, and you will never accomplish anything of lasting glory for God by using the devil's methods.

THE WEAPONS OF YOUR WARFARE

Some of your spiritual weapons are "guns," to be used in blowing away the enemy, and other weapons are "roses," sweet-smelling sacrifices to the Lord, which in turn result in a blessing to His people. The most important component in all these weapons is prayer. In one sense prayer is a weapon all by itself; in another way it is the "pipeline" through which all of the other weapons' powers are released. Prayer must be combined with faith. Jesus said, "Truly, truly, I say to you, he who believes in Me, the works that I do he will do also; and greater works than these he will do; because I go to the Father. Whatever you ask in My name, that will I do, so that the Father may be glorified in the Son. If you ask Me anything in My name, I will do it" (John 14:12–14).

What a tremendous promise Jesus has given to those who believe in Him. But please, if you don't believe in Jesus, or if you are tolerating willful sin in your life, don't attempt to engage in combat with the enemy. First, repent; get your own relationship with Jesus right. Saturate your mind with His Word by enlisting in some "basic training" Bible studies. Practice putting on the full armor of God before you go out to do battle with the devil. This is crucial because none of the weapons listed below will "work" without a vibrant, active faith in the One who empowers them.

THE NAME OF JESUS

Have you ever wondered why we pray in the name of Jesus? What does it mean to pray in Jesus's name, anyhow? For many Christians "in Jesus's name" is merely a signal that the prayer is almost over. It is a spiritual-sounding cap to put on our "McDonald's" prayers: "Lord, give me a hamburger and a Coke to go, and make it quick because I'm in a hurry. In Jesus's name, amen."

Tacking the name of Jesus on the end of your prayer is not necessarily praying in Jesus's name. To pray in His name means to pray in agreement with who Jesus is and what He wants to do in the world. Simply put, it is praying the same thing Jesus would pray. When we use Jesus's name that way, it carries the full power and authority of the risen Lord Jesus Christ.

Imagine you are driving down the highway when suddenly you hear a shrill, piercing sound. Your first response is to check your radio or sound system; no, everything is OK there. Then you glance in your rearview mirror and see a car with pretty red or blue lights flashing on its roof. You pull over, and the police car does the same, stopping behind you. The officer approaches your auto, taps on the window, and says, "Open up in the name of the law."

Now what causes you to open your window? Was it the siren? The flashing lights? The officer's decorum? All of the above? The clincher, of course, is that when the policeman says "in the name of the law," you know he has the full authority of the town, city, or state he represents. As such, if you are smart, you will do what the officer says.

Similarly when you are confronting any demonic entity, you must use the name of Jesus as a spiritual weapon. The devil and his demons hate the name of Jesus because it reminds them of all that He is and all that they are not. Nevertheless, Satan and his assistants know what the name of Jesus represents. The name of Jesus carries awesome authority in the spirit world because He has all authority in heaven. The name of Jesus is not a magic formula. But when used properly by a Spirit-filled believer, the name of Jesus sets the demons to flight.

Whose Authority Is It, Anyhow?

The real issue in every area of spiritual warfare is authority—who is in charge here? The devil loves to give the impression that he is the one calling the shots. He attempts to strike fear into our hearts by pouring out a raft of graphically, sensationalized, horror-evoking escapades. But the devil is a liar. If you read the Bible, you'll get a much different description of the devil and his demons and their activities. And not a line of it will cause you to have nightmares.

Why? Because in every confrontation with the devil or other

evil spirits, it is obvious that Jesus is "Master of the Universe." He is the one with real authority.

In Mark 5:1–17 you can find a clear illustration of this. Jesus had barely gotten out of the boat after crossing the Sea of Galilee when He encountered a deranged, demon-possessed man. Many scholars believe the man was inhabited by twelve thousand demons, as his name, Legion, may imply. Can you imagine that? Twelve thousand demons! *One* demon is too many.

No wonder this man was such a mess—so much so that society had written him off as a hopeless case. People had tried to tame him by binding him up with chains and clamping him down with shackles, but when the demonic spirits surged through the man's body, he chucked the chains and splintered the shackles as if they were made of string. Finally, polite, sophisticated society said, "There's nothing more that we can do with him," so the people threw him out of town to live among the tombs.

That's where Jesus found him, living among the dead in the local graveyard. The man was a raving maniac; he was naked, running around day and night, screaming insanely, and angrily cutting himself with jagged rocks.

Jesus could have passed by and simply ignored the poor fellow's plight. But He didn't. He wasn't repulsed by the man's obnoxious behavior. Neither was He afraid. Jesus understood that it was the demons within the man causing him to be so diabolical.

Jesus took command, exercising His own authority, and cast the spirits out of the man. He even patronized the demons a little by allowing them to enter a large herd of hogs. The pigs, all two thousand of them, promptly responded by rampaging down the mountain and drowning in the sea. But don't miss the point. Look who is in charge here. Certainly not the demons. They have to go where Jesus tells them. He is the Master. He is Lord.

Unfortunately the local population missed the point. When

the unbelieving townspeople heard the report of two thousand pigs taking the plunge, they came running out of town to see Jesus and to find out what had happened. When they arrived, the formerly possessed fellow was sitting there, clothed and in his right mind. The townspeople's reaction is interesting and surprisingly contemporary. They became afraid and asked Jesus to leave. The unbelievers in that town preferred to put up with demons rather than the supernatural power of Jesus. Some things never change.

Throughout the gospel accounts, in one situation after another, Jesus proved that His authority was greater than Satan's. His disciples watched, listened, and learned from Him as He cast out the evil spirits wherever He went. Then, finally, it was their turn. Jesus sent them on a "trial run."

Jesus sent out seventy of His followers, two by two, into every city He planned to visit. The seventy were sort of His "advance" men, preparing the way for Him. Jesus gave them similar instructions as those He gave to his closest disciples. He told them: "And as you go, preach, saying, 'The kingdom of heaven is at hand.' Heal the sick, raise the dead, cleanse the lepers, cast out demons. Freely you received, freely give" (Matt. 10:7–8).

Although Luke's account of the seventy's instructions includes only healing and preaching (Luke 10:9), apparently the disciples did more than that. The seventy returned to Jesus and excitedly reported, "Lord, even the demons are subject to us in Your name" (v. 17).

Jesus did not deny their report or squelch their enthusiasm in any way. In fact, it is easy to imagine a hint of a smile on Jesus's face as He said, "I was watching Satan fall from heaven like lightning" (v. 18). Then Jesus goes on to explain: "Behold, I have given you authority to tread upon serpents and scorpions, and over all the power of the enemy, and nothing will injure you. Nevertheless do not rejoice in this, that the spirits are subject to you, but rejoice that your names are recorded in heaven" (vv. 19–20).

Notice that Jesus has given to us, as His followers, the authority to engage in spiritual warfare and emerge victorious. It is delegated authority. It is authority in His name. Our authority is not on the basis of our strong personality types (or weak ones); nor does it have anything to do with our talent or skills, or how we feel, how we look, or even how long we have been serving the Lord. It is authority granted to us by Jesus Christ Himself to use His name to defeat the powers of darkness.

Now it is up to us to use the authority Jesus has given us. If we don't, the devil will go unchallenged. Jesus is not going to send an angel to do what He has already commissioned and empowered us to do. In his book *Spiritual Warfare for Every Christian*, Dean Sherman offers a whimsical insight regarding how foolish it is for Christians to neglect using their delegated authority:

> What if I were to arrive home and find people stealing my possessions? I call the police from my car phone and they rush over to my house. But to my surprise, they line up along the sidewalk and begin to sing about their authority, declaring it to one another. All the while, intruders finish cleaning out my house! This may seem ridiculous, yet that is often an accurate picture of what we do. We talk about our authority. We sing about it. We even proclaim it loudly. But we don't exercise it. We must recognize that there is a difference between having authority and using it.[1]

We need to learn how to take authority over the devil and his demons, using the authority that Jesus has delegated to us. When a young missionary by the name of Miss Mitchell learned how to stand in the authority of Christ, it literally saved her life.

Miss Mitchell grew up in Los Angeles, and it was the thrill

of her life to be appointed as a missionary to India. She couldn't wait to get there and to start telling the Indian people about Jesus.

Once Miss Mitchell arrived on the mission field, however, she quickly discovered that a world of difference separates studying to be a missionary and being one. Her first assignment was to assist two elderly female missionaries whose entire lives had been wrapped up in their work. Miss Mitchell couldn't relate to them, and they weren't eager to relate to her. An intense loneliness began to wrap around the young woman's heart.

Even more exasperating, she experienced great difficulty learning the language of the Indian people to whom she had come to minister. She couldn't understand them, and they couldn't understand her. Her sense of isolation caused her to become terribly homesick. She grew so miserable that she began to hate the Indian people—the very people she had left her home in the United States and traveled halfway around the world to win to Christ!

The final blow came when she became sick with amoebic dysentery. The doctor told Miss Mitchell that she would not get well if she stayed in India. Moreover, she would probably die if she didn't return home and get immediate medical attention.

The young missionary was brokenhearted, but she had no choice. She packed her suitcase and prepared to return home.

At nine o'clock on the morning she was scheduled to leave. She was having her "quiet time" with the Lord, just as she did every day. She read a passage of Scripture from Joshua 10 about the five warring kings who fled from Joshua and attempted to hide in a cave. But Joshua could not be fooled. He had his soldiers roll large stones in front of the cave, trapping the kings inside. Then Joshua continued pursuing the enemy and slaughtered the armies of the five kings. When he was satisfied that the enemy foot soldiers had been destroyed, Joshua turned his attention to the five kings in the cave.

Joshua commanded the cave to be opened and the five kings brought out to him. He then called his chief warriors and told them to put their feet on the necks of the five enemy kings. While his captains stood upon the enemies' necks, Joshua said, "Do not fear or be dismayed! Be strong and courageous, for thus the LORD will do to all your enemies with whom you fight" (Josh. 10:25). Then Joshua put the enemy kings to death and hung them on trees for all to see.

As Miss Mitchell read this account, she realized that she too had five enemies: her loneliness, her problems with the Indian language, her sense of isolation and homesickness, her lack of love for the Indian people, and her physical sickness. She felt as though these five enemies were attacking her and threatening to end her ministry as a missionary.

Miss Mitchell decided to assert her God-given authority. Why should she have to go back home in defeat? Didn't she trust in the living Lord Jesus? Didn't He have all authority? Had she not forsaken all to follow Him? Had she not traveled all the way to India for the sake of the call, because of faith in His name and on the basis of His authority?

Miss Mitchell got angry at what Satan was attempting to do to her. She took five pieces of paper and wrote on each of them the name of one of her five enemies. On one she wrote, "Loneliness," on another, "Language," and so on until she had named specifically all five. She threw the papers on the floor and acted upon her decision to take authority over her circumstances. She put her foot on one "enemy" after the other, proclaiming aloud, "In the name of my all-powerful, resurrected Lord, I take authority over you and declare you defeated!" In a further act of faith Miss Mitchell unpacked her suitcase and told the mission leaders she was staying, come what may.

The work of the Lord on her behalf was almost immediate. That same day she found a teacher who could help her with the language. A short time after that she met an American man in India. He too was able to help her learn the Indian language and adapt to India's customs. As they spent more time together, the young missionary's loneliness disappeared. She was becoming adept at the Indian language and found her love growing stronger for the Indian people. As a result her homesickness disappeared as well. She and her American friend fell in love and married. Amazingly she was also healed of her physical infirmity!

Granted, not every account of spiritual warfare has such a fairy-tale ending, but the point is, the devil would have driven Miss Mitchell home in defeat and most likely out of the ministry had she not learned how to take authority over her devilish enemies in the all-powerful name of her Lord Jesus Christ.[2]

NOW IT'S YOUR TURN

You will want to learn how to do something similar, using the authority Jesus has given you in His name. Maybe you have fewer than five "enemy kings" trying to intimidate you; maybe you have more than five. Perhaps you are living in fear, frustration, or defeat. Possibly Satan has been piercing your armor with his fiery darts, and you have been feeling helpless and hopeless to defend yourself. Or maybe the devil has had you on the run because of guilt, false accusations (or even accurate accusations), painful childhood memories, feelings of futility in the present, and no hope for a fruitful future.

Whatever your circumstances, consider a few questions:

- Do you trust in the Lord Jesus Christ as your Savior? If the answer is yes, say, "Yes!" out loud right now. (If you are reading this book in a library or doctor's office, it's OK to whisper, but say it aloud. Speak it out so the devil and his demons can hear you.)

- Do you believe that your living Lord Jesus has all authority in heaven and on earth (Matt. 28:18)? Then say, "Yes, I believe Jesus has all authority in heaven and on earth."

- Do you believe He has given you the privilege of praying and the authority to use His name? You know what to do.

If you believe these things, then in the name of Jesus, stand up, take your position of authority in His name, and place your foot upon the necks of the "enemies" that have been plaguing your life. You may wish to do as Miss Mitchell did and write the names on a piece of paper, place your foot on each one, and declare that enemy defeated in the name of Jesus. As you do, speak aloud, "All authority in heaven and earth belongs to Jesus. I am His, and He is mine. Christ Jesus is alive in me. Therefore, all authority in His name is mine, and I now declare you ('enemies,' demons, or Satan himself) defeated. I praise God for this victory right now."

Then take the next step of obedience that God directs you to take. For Miss Mitchell, her act of faith and obedience was unpacking her suitcase in the face of her doctor's dire predictions. Your next step of faith, of course, will depend upon your personal situation. Whatever it is that demonstrates your faith and obedience, do it.

The matter of taking spiritual authority in Jesus's name is so essential to your success in spiritual warfare that it merits more discussion. It is time to show you how to set the devil and his demons to flight.

Chapter Thirteen

DEMONS ON THE RUN

O NE OF SATAN'S greatest fears is that you will realize the incredible authority you have in the name of Jesus. The devil knows that Jesus dealt him a decisive blow on the cross at Calvary. When Jesus said, "It is finished," the prophecies were fulfilled concerning His sacrificial death, which made possible our salvation. Besides that, it was doomsday for the devil and his demons. It was all over.

Years later the apostle John reminded his readers about the twofold purpose for Jesus's coming to earth: "You know that He appeared in order to take away sins.... The Son of God appeared for this purpose, to destroy the works of the devil" (1 John 3:5, 8). That is exactly what Jesus did by dying on the cross. He paid the price for our sins, and He destroyed the works of the devil; He broke sin's power. Jesus reclaimed the authority that Satan had stolen from Adam and Eve long ago, and He gave it to all who believe in Him.

The Bible says, "But as many as received Him, to them He gave the right to become children of God, even to those who believe in His name" (John 1:12). The word *right* also means "authority" or "it is lawful." In other words, Jesus was saying it is perfectly right for those who believe in Him to assume all the privileges and authority that come with being a child of God. Because Jesus has all authority in heaven and on earth, and He lives in us, that means *we* have all authority too. Our authority, of course, is derived from His.

Power in the Name of Jesus

Always remember that your authority is delegated to you by Jesus. His allowing you to use His authority is similar to you allowing one of your children to borrow the family car. In one sense the car belongs to your child because your son or daughter is part of the family. Yet in another sense the car is not his or hers; it is yours. It is registered in your name, and out of the kindness of your heart you are allowing your son or daughter to use it. You expect your children to obey the law and use the vehicle in the same manner as you would. You are entrusting him or her with the keys, but it is still your car.

In a similar way, before Jesus ascended to heaven He told His disciples, "All authority has been given to Me in heaven and on earth. Go therefore and make disciples of all the nations, baptizing them in the name of the Father and the Son and the Holy Spirit, teaching them to observe all that I commanded you; and lo, I am with you always, even to the end of the age" (Matt. 28:18–20). In the parallel account Mark quotes Jesus as saying that those who believe and are baptized will have signs accompany them, miracles that testify to their faith. Jesus said, "In My name they will cast out demons, they will speak with new tongues; they will pick up serpents, and if they drink any deadly poison, it will not hurt them; they will lay hands on the sick, and they will recover" (Mark 16:17–18).

Bible scholars have spent years debating whether the material in Mark 16:9–20 is an accurate representation of the best and earliest manuscripts of Mark's Gospel. Nevertheless, some groups associated with Christianity have insisted upon using this passage of Scripture as a litmus test of their faith. They have purposely picked up live, poisonous snakes, and some have willfully imbibed poisonous drinks...and have lived! Regardless of the textual criticism or the wisdom (or lack of it) of testing your faith against potentially lethal activities, the truth of the matter

146

is, the early disciples did all of the things Jesus mentioned in Mark 16:15–18 except drink deadly poison. (Considering the rancid water supply in Rome and parts of the Middle East, many of them may have done that too.)

Jesus's disciples prophesied in His name (Matt. 7:22). They cast out demons in His name (Luke 10:17). They performed many miracles of healing in His name. They did all sorts of spiritual exploits in the powerful name of Jesus. The early disciples recognized and understood that the name of Jesus and the person of Jesus are for all practical purposes inseparable. They are one, the same. When you say, "In the name of Jesus," you are really saying, "In the person and power of Jesus Christ, King of kings and Lord of lords!" Now that's powerful.

CAN'T STOP TALKING ABOUT JESUS

One of my favorite illustrations of this is in Acts chapters 3 and 4. In Acts 3:1 Peter and John were going up to the Jewish temple to pray when they encountered a lame beggar sitting outside one of the main gates to the temple area. The beggar hit on Peter and John, asking them for a few bucks to support his favorite charity—himself. But Peter and John looked him right in the eyes, and Peter said, "I do not possess silver and gold, but what I do have I give to you: In the name of Jesus Christ the Nazarene—walk!" (v. 6).

There it is again: "In the name of Jesus!" And the guy got up and walked. Actually, he did much more than walk. He began "walking and leaping and praising God" all the way into the temple, along with Peter and John (v. 8). The local worshippers all recognized the beggar, and they were amazed that he had been healed (v. 10). After all, the man was over forty years of age (Acts 4:22), and he probably had been crippled most or all of those years. No doubt he had become a "fixture" outside the gate of the temple. People pitied him—contributing a few coins for his care or despising him, avoiding his desperate, despairing stare. Now here he was, right in the temple of the Lord, dancing and praising God. Did the people notice? Count on it.

Peter, hot off his power-packed sermon on the Day of Pentecost after which three thousand people committed their lives to Christ, sensed a perfect opportunity to preach. He told the crowd:

> Men of Israel, why are you amazed at this, or why do you gaze at us, as if by our own power or piety we had made him walk? The God of Abraham, Isaac and Jacob, the God of our fathers, has glorified His servant Jesus...the one whom God raised from the dead, a fact to which we are witnesses.
>
> And on the basis of faith in His name, it is the name of Jesus which has strengthened this man whom you see and know; and the faith which comes through Him has given him this perfect health in the presence of you all.
>
> —ACTS 3:12–13, 15–16

The captain of the temple guard and some of the Sadducees, a Jewish sect that did not believe in the resurrection of the dead, were not exactly thrilled with Peter's message. They grabbed Peter and John and hauled them into prison for telling people about Jesus. The next day Peter and John were called to give an account of themselves before Annas, Caiaphas, John, and Alexander, the same chief priests who had condemned Jesus to death less than two months earlier.

The Jewish rulers asked Peter and John a loaded question: "By what power, or in what name, have you done this?" (Acts 4:7). Notice, the Jewish leaders did not attempt to discount the authenticity of the miracle. They had tried that approach with the resurrection of Jesus and had failed miserably. Nevertheless,

148

after nearly two months of relative peace and quiet in Jerusalem, the Jewish rulers had reason to believe that everything was getting back to normal. But then, on the Day of Pentecost, all heaven had broken loose, and now here were these two men going around healing people in the name of Jesus. The Jewish leaders must have thought, "Oh, no! Not again!"

The first part of the question they asked pertained to the power behind the miracle. They may have been accusing Peter and John of performing "black" magic, insinuating that the healing of the crippled man had a demonic source.

The second part of their question was concerning the "name" behind the miracle. To the Jews, to use somebody's name in a miraculous manner implied that the person to whom the name belonged had authority over, or responsibility for, the person upon whom the miracle was performed. (For examples of this, see 2 Samuel 12:28; Psalm 49:11; Isaiah 4:1.) Nevertheless, the Jewish rulers were not expecting Peter's response: "Let it be known to all of you and to all the people of Israel, that by the name of Jesus Christ the Nazarene, whom you crucified, whom God raised from the dead—by this name this man stands here before you in good health....And there is salvation in no one else; for there is no other name under heaven that has been given among men by which we must be saved" (Acts 4:10, 12).

No doubt the Jewish chief priests just about tossed their turbans at that! Peter was saying precisely what they did not want to hear. Still, the priests could not deny that something was different about these guys...but what was it? Then it hit them: "As they observed the confidence of Peter and John and understood that they were uneducated and untrained men, they were amazed, and began to recognize them as having been with Jesus" (v. 13).

I love that part of the story. Can't you just imagine those stuffy, old chief priests' expressions as they listened to Peter's words?

No doubt they wondered, "Who are these jokers anyhow? How dare they say such things to us, the cream of the religious crop? Who do these guys think they are?"

But then they began to recognize them as having been with Jesus.

"Where do they get their confidence?

"They have been with Jesus."

"How do they know so much? They've never gone to Bible school or seminary. How can they understand these things?"

"They have been with Jesus."

"Where did they get such supernatural power?"

"They have been with Jesus."

That says it all, doesn't it? They have been with Jesus. They have been spending time in His presence. They are filled with His Holy Spirit and convinced that Jesus Christ is alive from the dead. They are unstoppable!

The Jewish leaders realized they could not deny the miracle or the fact that it had taken place through Peter and John in the name of Jesus, so they threatened them, commanding Peter and John "not to speak or teach at all in the name of Jesus. But Peter and John answered and said to them, 'Whether it is right in the sight of God to give heed to you rather than to God, you be the judge; for we cannot stop speaking what we have seen and heard'" (vv. 18–20).

Peter and John basically answered, "Hey, guys; you can do whatever you want to us; you can threaten us, beat us, throw us in jail again; you could even kill us. But we can't stop talking about Jesus and what He has done for us." The Jewish rulers threatened the disciples further and finally released them because the people of Jerusalem were glorifying God for what had happened.

Power to Protect You

Songwriter Gary S. Paxton discovered early in his Christian life that there is enough power in the name of Jesus to protect us from direct assaults of the enemy. Gary was working in his Nashville recording studio one night when two men knocked on his door. Their car had broken down. The problem was a dead battery, they thought, so they asked to use Gary's telephone. Gary kindly offered to jump-start the guys' car from his van. The men agreed, and the three of them piled into Gary's vehicle.

Gary had no sooner gotten behind the wheel when the guys jumped him. One of the men put a "hammerlock" hold on Gary and jerked him backward in the driver's seat. The other man pulled a gun.

Gary immediately began screaming at the men, "In the name of Jesus, you can't kill me! In the name of Jesus, you can't kill me!" The men tried, but they couldn't kill Gary. They wrestled violently in the front seat of the van, and the gun went off several times. Gary was hit, and so was one of the thugs. They all tumbled out of the van onto the street.

One of the assailants later said he had a perfect opportunity to shoot Gary in the head, but he was unable to pull the trigger. Instead he threw the gun into a thicket and ran away, leaving his blood-soaked buddy lying in the street. Gary was severely wounded, but he lived. He was able to identify his assailants, and the men went to prison.[1] To this day Gary says had he not immediately begun defending himself with the name of Jesus, he would probably be dead.

This Is Not Magic

To use the name of Jesus effectively against the devil and his demons, you must know Jesus Christ personally and have an active relationship with Him. Remember, His name represents

His person. You cannot simply shout, "In the name of Jesus!", at the devil and expect him to flee if you do not have a relationship with Christ or if your relationship has been fractured by willful sin.

The seven sons of Sceva, a Jewish chief priest, attempted to do just that and were lucky to escape with their lives. Sceva's sons were Jewish exorcists who went from town to town, ostensibly casting out evil spirits, although in actuality they were probably putting on more of a "religious show" than anything else and bilking the people. No doubt they were dabbling in "black magic" and other occult practices.

When they heard that God was performing great miracles through the apostle Paul in the name of Jesus, they decided to get in on the action. Like many people today, these guys thought they could just use the right words and bring about the desired effect. They wanted to use Paul's methods without his source of power—the Holy Spirit. Either that or they simply did not understand the sort of powers with which they were playing. They attempted to cast out an evil spirit in the name of the Lord Jesus, saying, "I adjure you by Jesus whom Paul preaches" (Acts 19:13).

What the exorcists said was OK, but the evil spirit was totally unimpressed. Why? The exorcists' words were empty and hollow. Sceva's sons lacked the authority and power of Jesus because they did not have a relationship with Jesus. There is no power in the name of Jesus apart from the person of Jesus.

It is ironic that these guys were sons of a Jewish chief priest. They had probably grown up with the Scriptures being read around their house. They should have known better. Similarly you can be the son or daughter of a chief priest, a pastor, evangelist, elder, deacon, or Sunday school teacher, but if you do not know Jesus personally and have His Spirit working in you, the devil will stomp all over you. That's exactly what happened to the sons of Sceva.

Unafraid of these fakers, the demon spoke almost sarcastically, "I recognize Jesus, and I know about Paul, but who are you?" (Acts 19:15). *Whoom!* The evil spirit smacked Sceva's sons right in the face with the truth. "Who are you to come around here messing with me under your own power? You have no authority in the spirit realm. You have no spiritual power. You don't represent Jesus to me. Why, you foolish frauds, I'm gonna rip your faces off!"

At that point the Scripture records: "And the man, in whom was the evil spirit, leaped on them and subdued all of them and overpowered them, so that they fled out of that house naked and wounded" (v. 16).

That is a nice way of saying that the demon beat the living daylights out of Sceva's sons! Now notice the results of this strange incident.

Fear fell on Ephesus.

Ephesus was a city obsessed with the occult. Once a thriving seaport, it was a town in which the presence of Satan was welcomed and the practices of sorcery and magic were not only prevalent but were also publicly sanctioned and practiced openly. Ephesus was the center for the worship of Artemis (sometimes called "Diana" in the New Testament), a female fertility goddess.

The infamous temple of Artemis was located in the city, so all kinds of weird, demonically inspired priests and priestesses constantly congregated in Ephesus. As such, Ephesus was swarming with male and female prostitutes, soothsayers, magicians, and sorcerers, all vying for the attention and the money of the local population and the city's many visitors.

But when the people of Ephesus learned the details about the demon's defiant defeat of the seven sons of Sceva as well as the miracles done through Paul, an awesome fear fell upon the city (Acts 19:17). It was the same sort of awesome, reverential fear that fell upon the early church in the city of Jerusalem when God snuffed out Ananias and Sapphira for lying to the Holy Spirit (Acts 5:11).

Jesus's name was magnified.

One of the oddest results of a demon beating up on a couple of occult practitioners was that "the name of the Lord Jesus was being magnified" (Acts 19:17). Not that God desires demons or anyone else to go around pummeling people so the name of Jesus can be exalted. No, clearly the people of Ephesus recognized genuine spiritual power being manifested through the apostle Paul, as opposed to the spiritual impotence of the occult priests. That is why the name of Jesus was being magnified. Similarly the name of Jesus *will* be exalted in your town or situation, no matter how demon-infested it is.

Sin was confessed.

So impressed were the Ephesians at this obvious display of Paul's spiritual superiority through the power of Jesus's name that they began to confess and disclose their sinful practices (v. 18). No doubt many of them were involved in the worship of Artemis and flagrant sexual immorality, which was standard practice within the cult. Confronted by the power of the Jesus, they began to cast off their false and impure worship.

Magic books were burned.

As part of the practical results of these people's repentance, they abandoned anything that was an abomination to God. Once they realized the error of their ways, they renounced anything from their pasts that might impede their spiritual progress. "And many of those who practiced magic brought their books together and began burning them in the sight of everyone; and they counted up the price of them and found it fifty thousand pieces of silver" (v. 19).

Frequently when modern-day believers realize the potential danger and damage demonically inspired books, magazines movies, music, video games, or other vehicles laced with destructive content represent to their spiritual lives, they decide to have a bonfire too. If you have literature, videos, or music in your possession that glorify the devil or exalt a lifestyle that is contrary to the Bible and your relationship with Jesus, take a tip from these new converts from demon worship. Trash the trash before it trashes you.

Notice too that the new converts were not concerned about the cost of their black magic books and materials. Nowadays many Christians rationalize, "I know it is counterproductive to my spiritual health, but I paid a lot of money for those books and CDs. I can't afford to throw them away."

Can you afford to give the enemy an open door into your life? You can't afford not to destroy those demonically oriented materials. Destroy them. Don't give them to other people so the devil can use the dirt in their lives too.

God's Word goes forth.

As a result of this encounter, "the word of the Lord was growing mightily and prevailing" (v. 20). The message of Jesus spread throughout the city. But don't think the devil took this defeat lying down. Oh, no! Acts 19:23 says it succinctly: "About that time there occurred no small disturbance concerning the Way." Many people in Ephesus made a good living by handcrafting idols of Artemis to be sold to the locals and the visitors to the pagan city. But people who meet Jesus don't buy idols (or at least, they shouldn't), and a silversmith named Demetrius quickly recognized the threat to their business and stirred up a riot against Paul. Nevertheless, despite the opposition of people who wished to use religion for their own personal profit, the Word of the Lord continued to prevail. It always will.

GETTING THE NAME RIGHT

If you don't know Jesus Christ, or if you are not living in a right relationship with Him, again I strongly caution you: never attempt to deal with the devil in any way. It could be extremely hazardous to your health. Not even the mighty archangel Michael would speak against the devil in his own strength. The Bible says Michael "did not dare pronounce against him a railing judgment, but said, 'The Lord rebuke you'" (Jude 9).

If you do not know Jesus, or if you have allowed sin to drive a wedge in your relationship with Him, call out His name; beg Him for forgiveness of your sins; ask Him to come and fill you with His Holy Spirit. Commit yourself to trusting Him and obeying His Word for the rest of your life. Only then do you have the right (legal authority) to use His name against the devil.

If you *do* know Jesus, you need to learn how to properly use His name as a weapon in spiritual warfare. Some people say, "In the name of Jesus, whom the pastor preaches about...!"

That's not good enough.

Others say, "In the name of Jesus, whom Mom and Dad told me about..."

That won't cut it either.

"In the name of Jesus whom we sing about..."

Not good enough.

"In the name of Jesus that I read about..."

No. It is not the name of Jesus you need to know; it is the person and power of Jesus Christ in you that is necessary to take authority over the devil. You need to be able to declare with confidence, before friend or foe, angel or demon:

"In the name of Jesus, my Savior and Lord!"

"In the name of Jesus, the Lamb of God who takes away the sin of the world!"

"In the name of Jesus, who came to destroy the works of the devil!"

"In the name of Jesus, my healer!"

"My deliverer!"

"My provider!"

"My shield and my strength!"

"My shepherd!"

"My peace!"

"My rock!"

"My righteousness!"

"My redeemer!"

"The Holy One! The Mighty One! The Lord of hosts!"

"In the name of Jesus Christ, King of kings and Lord of lords!"

That is who He is, and that is the name that causes the devil and his demons to tremble. The name of Jesus is not a magic formula you pull out of your bag of tricks to impress your friends or to put on some sort of spiritual sideshow. Yes, there is power in the name of Jesus, but that power can be used properly and effectively only by a Spirit-filled believer who is living daily in Jesus's presence and operating in the delegated authority He has given you.

God is not about to entrust His power and authority to anyone less committed to Him. After all, you would not trust a stack of dynamite and a box of matches to a pyromaniac. Nor would you allow a thief to guard a bank. Neither is God going to entrust His supernatural power and authority to someone whose allegiance and motives are questionable.

The name of Jesus is a powerful weapon in spiritual warfare, but only when it is wielded by a person who speaks His name with Christ's delegated authority. Yes, you can speak the name of Jesus with boldness, but always remember it is not your power that drives out the demons; it is His.

Chapter Fourteen

POWER TO BIND, POWER TO LOOSE, POWER TO SPARE!

ONE OF THE truly astonishing weapons Jesus has entrusted to us is the permission to "bind and loose" things in His name. Jesus told Peter, "I will give you the keys of the kingdom of heaven; and whatever you bind on earth shall have been bound in heaven, and whatever you loose on earth shall have been loosed in heaven" (Matt. 16:19).

This is one of those incredible, enigmatic, "almost-too-good-to-be-true" promises of Jesus. When you first read it, you tend to think, "Naah! Surely Jesus does not really mean this promise for me. It must be for some spiritually elite group, or perhaps it applied only to the original apostles. Certainly Jesus knows better than to entrust such awesome authority to me!"

But then, almost as if to make sure we don't miss the point, Jesus repeats the promise verbatim in Matthew 18:18. He adds there: "Again I say to you, that if two of you agree on earth about anything that they may ask, it shall be done for them by My Father who is in heaven. For where two or three have gathered together in My name, I am there in their midst" (Matt. 18:19–20).

There it is again: Ask anything *in My name*.

But what does it mean to bind and loose in Jesus's name? The biblical word for *bind* means "to tie up." Positively speaking, it can mean to tie up an enemy or a thief who has been caught.

Negatively the enemy attempts to tie God's people in knots. These believers need to be "loosed," or set free. Jesus said in Matthew 12:29, "How can anyone enter the strong man's house and carry off his property, unless he first binds the strong man. And then he will plunder his house." With this truth in mind C. Peter Wagner says, "In the context of spiritual warfare, binding means restricting the power of evil on all levels."[1]

"Loosing" is the process of untying the cords of bondage in which a person has been constricted. One of the best examples of "loosing" in the New Testament is when Jesus raised Lazarus from the dead. Jesus called Lazarus to newness of life, and Lazarus got out of his grave and came forth. But he was still bound hand and foot by the bandages that had been used for his embalming. Even his face remained wrapped in the grave cloth (John 11:44). He looked worse than Boris Karloff in the old horror flick *The Mummy*.

Can you imagine what a miserable existence Lazarus would have had if Jesus had left him in that condition? Sure, Lazarus was alive, but he could barely move, talk, or breathe, and he certainly wasn't having much fun. Sounds like a lot of Christians!

In his sermon "I Talk Back to the Devil" A. W. Tozer comments upon this condition:

> Why doesn't the old devil, Satan, give up and bow out of the picture when a person becomes a believing Christian? Although he is a dark and sinister foe dedicated to the damnation of humans, I think he knows that it is no use trying to damn a forgiven and justified child of God who is in the Lord's hands.
>
> So, it becomes the devil's business to keep the Christian's spirit imprisoned. He knows that the believing and justified Christian has been raised up out of the grave of his sins and trespasses. From that point

on, Satan works that much harder to keep us bound and gagged, actually imprisoned in our own grave clothes.

He knows that if we continue in this kind of bondage, we will never be able to claim our rightful spiritual heritage. He knows also that while we continue bound in this kind of enslavement we are not much better off than when we were spiritually dead.[2]

But Jesus was not content to allow Lazarus to remain as one of the "walking dead." Jesus commanded the onlookers, friends, and family members, "Unbind him, and let him go" (John 11:44).

Have you ever thought about that? Why didn't Jesus release Lazarus from the cords of bondage when He raised him from the dead? He could have done so with just a word. But He didn't. He left the loosing process to the close friends and family members of Lazarus. I believe He was also teaching us a lesson.

Many times people come to "newness of life" in Jesus, but they are still bound by things from their past. Perhaps they are still struggling with bad habits formed over many years of living without Jesus, habits such as alcoholism, drug addictions, sexual sins, or other evil practices. Others come into the kingdom of God with all sorts of hurt, bitterness, and resentment from their past. Still others are plagued by deep-seated fear, loneliness, or doubts.

Granted, when we repent of our sins, we turn away from those things, but sometimes people need a bit of help from their brothers and sisters in the Lord to help unbind them. Not that we can bring anyone to newness of life or take away a single sin, but we may be instruments the Lord can use to encourage the freedom He wants all believers to experience through the process of sanctification (being made holy, filled with His Spirit, and set apart for His purposes).

In many cases it is necessary to bind "the strong man" (the satanic influences) in a person's life before you can minister to him or her in any other way. How can we do this? Through prayer in the name of Jesus. First, name that thing (or things) that is tying up or hindering the person for whom you are praying. It may be a habit, an attitude, or some demonic intimidation such as a spirit of fear. Acknowledge that from this point on Jesus is Lord in its place.

Second, bind up that "strong man" in the name of Jesus. For example, let's say it is a spirit of fear you are coming against in prayer. You know that such a spirit is not from God. The Bible says, "There is no fear in love; but perfect love casts out fear" (1 John 4:18). Use the Scriptures as your sword and speak directly to the spirit of fear, saying something such as: "On the authority of God's Word and in the name of Jesus Christ, I bind you, spirit of fear. You shall no longer have dominion or presence in this life. In your place I loose the love of Jesus, the perfect love of His Holy Spirit."

It is helpful to speak aloud when binding or loosing something in Jesus's name. Say something such as, "Satan, I bind you in the name of Jesus!" Then proceed to speak words of release. Frequently it will be necessary to speak directly to the demonic entities. You need not yell or scream; simply use your delegated authority. "In the name of Jesus Christ, King of kings and Lord of lords, unbind this person and let him (or her) go!"

POWER TO SPARE YOUR LIFE

Sometimes it is necessary to bind the devil literally to save somebody's life. In the case of Darlene Cunningham, wife of Youth With A Mission president, Loren Cunningham, the life she saved was her own. Loren relates the story in his book *Making Jesus Lord*:

> One winter while we were living in Switzerland, Darlene reached behind an industrial-size washing machine to

retrieve a piece of laundry. She didn't know someone had been working on that machine and had left a protective cover off. Her hand touched a live electrical wire. She stood there with snow-covered shoes on a concrete floor, frozen to the exposed wires with her body pinned against the steel of the washer as 380 volts of electricity coursed through her body.

Darlene told me later that she screamed and screamed and no one heard her. She cried to the Lord to save her life, but still the jolts pounded through her. "Lord," she finally cried, "we've given our lives to you and I'm praying and it's not working!"

Instantly, God spoke to her. "Bind the devil."

Darlene knew what that meant. She bound the devil, praying against him in the authority of Jesus Christ (Matthew 16:19). As soon as she did, she was hurled off the live wire and slammed into the wall opposite the washing machine. For several days she experienced heart palpitations and weakness and the hole burned in the palm of her hand took months to heal. But she was all right.[3]

WHEN BINDING AND LOOSING DOESN'T WORK

In most books on the subject of spiritual warfare you will find a plethora of fascinating stories describing tremendous exploits done by ordinary believers decimating demonic strongholds. While I am greatly blessed and encouraged by these accounts, I would be less than honest with you if I did not make you aware that "binding and loosing" sometimes doesn't work. Why not?

First, admittedly we don't understand much about binding and loosing. The Bible contains few illustrations of how this weapon is to be used. Jesus did not teach a weekend seminar on the subject. He simply granted us the authority to do it as we find it necessary.

Second, sometimes we don't understand the sort of demonic powers with which we are dealing. As I've said throughout this book, demons play hardball. They have nothing to lose and nothing to gain. They will not receive a hotter or cooler spot in hell because of their success or failure rate. Their only pleasure, if you can call it that, is that misery loves company. If Satan can destroy you, that gives him a twisted sense of satisfaction in knowing that he has succeeded in keeping you from God.

Satan and his demons are not to be taken lightly. I cringe sometimes when I hear individuals irresponsibly or theatrically screaming at the devil in churches or on television, "I bind you, Satan, and your demons!" I can almost imagine some demons listening in and saying, "Hey, Wormwood; get a load of this guy screaming at us. What a weirdo, huh?"

Usually, however, when binding and loosing doesn't work, it is because we are trying to bind or loose something that Jesus does not intend to be bound or loosed. In other words, we must bind or loose in sync with Jesus in heaven.

For example, if I say, "I bind you, Satan, and cast you into a lake of fire for a thousand years," I am not showing my spiritual boldness but my spiritual ignorance. The simple fact is, Satan is not going to be bound and thrown into a lake of fire until Jesus does it (Rev. 20:10). For me to attempt to do so is foolish and possibly even dangerous. Satan laughs and says, "You silly boy. You don't know your Bible as well as I do."

On the other hand, when we oppose the devil and his demons in Jesus's name, praying with His authority according to His will, the devil's troops take off running. The devil knows when he is whipped, and he won't hang around.

Finally, when binding and loosing is ineffective, it may be

because we are not filled with the Holy Spirit, or perhaps we need to be "refilled." As a result, we're not operating completely under His power. Without the supernatural power of Jesus, we can bind and loose until we are blue in the face but to no avail. To the extent that we are or are not filled with the Spirit of Christ, we can expect a corresponding increase or reduction in spiritual power. That is why before we go any further, we better check the "fuel gauges."

Chapter Fifteen

THE DEVIL OR THE DOVE

I F YOU STUDY church history carefully, you will quickly discover that great Christians throughout the years have described some experience subsequent to their salvation through which they entered into a deeper relationship with Christ. The terms they used to describe this relationship vary widely, but if you examine the common denominators, you will discover that they were talking about a life surrendered to Jesus Christ and filled with His Spirit.

Their testimonies are not restricted to one time, place, race, sex, or church affiliation. Men and women from a broad spectrum, such as Hudson Taylor, D. L. Moody, Charles Finney, Corrie ten Boom, Oswald Chambers, Blaise Pascal, Phoebe Palmer, Andrew Murray, Ian Thomas, A. B. Simpson, Amy Carmichael, and a host of others all bear witness to an experience that took place at some point *after* they met Jesus Christ, an experience that revolutionized their *Christian* lives.

Dr. Ray Edman, former president and chancellor of Wheaton College, said about these "saints":

> The pattern of their experiences is much the same. They had believed on the Savior, yet they were burdened and bewildered, unfaithful and unfruitful, always yearning for a better way and never achieving by their effort a better life.[1]

Does that sound familiar to you? If so, you can be encouraged in knowing that darkness and defeat once described the lives of some of the church's most valiant heroes. Yet something happened to change them. What made the difference in their lives? Dr. Edman continues:

> They came to a crisis of utter heart surrender to the Savior, a meeting with Him in the innermost depths of their spirit; and they found the Holy Spirit to be an unfailing fountain of life and refreshment. Thereafter life was never the same.... Out of discouragement and defeat they have come into victory. Out of weakness and weariness they have been made strong. Out of ineffectiveness and apparent uselessness they have become efficient and enthusiastic.
>
> The pattern seems to be self-centeredness, self-effort, increasing inner dissatisfaction and outer discouragement, a temptation to give it all up because there is not a better way; and then finding the Spirit of God to be their strength, their guide, their confidence and companion—in a word, their life.[2]

WHAT ABOUT YOU?

Have you had such an infilling experience with the Holy Spirit? If not, you can—and you should! Let me emphasize that all true Christians have the Holy Spirit dwelling in them. In fact, to be a Christian, you *must* have the Spirit of God residing in you. Scripture says, "If anyone does not have the Spirit of Christ, he does not belong to Him" (Rom. 8:9).

The Bible also says, "The Spirit Himself testifies with our spirit that we are children of God" (v. 16). You can turn that around and say if the Spirit of God does not bear witness with your spirit, no matter how good a person you are, how often you go to church, or how much money you put in the offering, you are not a child of God. If the Spirit has not confirmed your reservation in the kingdom of God, you better establish a relationship with Jesus. Being a Christian isn't an "I think so" or an "I hope so" relationship. It is an "I know so" commitment. You commit your life to Jesus Christ, He commits Himself to you, and His Spirit bears witness with your spirit that you are a child of God. If that has not happened, you better go back to square one and start over.

If I asked, "Are you married?" you don't have to wonder, "Hmmm...am I married or not?" Or, "Well, I don't think I am married. I did go out on a date once, though. I'd like to be married. I've been considering marriage." That's ridiculous. You know the correct answer the moment I ask. It's either yes or no. Similarly if I ask you, "Are you a Christian?" you should be able to answer with equal certainty.

If you are trusting Jesus Christ as Savior, you have the Holy Spirit dwelling within you, and He will let you know somehow deep within your heart that you are a child of God. He probably won't make an announcement at work or display a sign on the blimp above the ball game, but you will know, just as the person who is married knows that he or she is married, not because of a marriage license but because of the public commitment that has been made.

When it comes to being filled with the Holy Spirit, the issue is not getting more of the Holy Spirit; it is the Holy Spirit getting all of you. You've probably seen some Christians who seem to have it together with God in a way that you don't. Their eyes have a bright sparkle, no matter what difficulties they are facing. They smile a lot. The joy of the Lord is something they don't have to conjure up, but it seems to come naturally to them.

As you consider those Christians, you may say, "They have something I don't have."

No, they don't have *something*. Something has *them*. Better still, *Someone* has them. These radiant Christians have surrendered their lives totally to Jesus Christ. He has cleansed their hearts and filled them with His Holy Spirit, and that has made all the difference in the world in their *Christian* lives.

WHO IS THE HOLY SPIRIT?

The Holy Spirit is not an angel, nor is He a tiny pixie like Tinkerbell in *Peter Pan*. Neither is He the Christian version of Casper the Friendly Ghost. He is the third Person of the Holy Trinity, which includes the Father, the Son (Jesus), and the Holy Spirit.

He existed and was active even before the formation of the earth (Gen. 1:2). Throughout the Old Testament times He empowered certain individuals to accomplish specific tasks. For example, God filled a man named Bezalel with the Holy Spirit and gave him great wisdom, understanding, and knowledge in craftsmanship to help oversee the construction of the first tabernacle (Exod. 31:2–5). Moses was also filled with God's Spirit, as were Gideon, Saul, David, and others. In Old Testament times, however, only a few of God's people were filled with the Holy Spirit, and then only for specific purposes.

In the New Testament the Holy Spirit's role is much more prominent. The night before Jesus went to the cross, He explained to His disciples that He had to go away for a while. Understandably the disciples were confused, sorrowful, and disappointed. But Jesus encouraged them by saying, "I will ask the Father, and He will give you another Helper, that He may be with you forever; that is the Spirit of truth, whom the world cannot receive, because it does not see Him or know Him, but you know Him because He abides with you and will be in you. I will not leave you as orphans; I will come to you" (John 14:16–18).

The word *Helper* that Jesus used to refer to the Holy Spirit means "one called alongside of, a Comforter."[3] That's who the

Holy Spirit is; He is a support upon which you can lean. He is the one who brings Jesus's peace and comfort to your heart and mind.

Jesus explained specifically what the Holy Spirit's role would be: "The Helper, the Holy Spirit, whom the Father will send in My name, He will teach you all things, and bring to your remembrance all that I said to you....When the Helper comes, whom I will send to you from the Father, that is the Spirit of truth who proceeds from the Father, He will testify about Me" (John 14:26; 15:26).

Why Did Jesus Have to Leave?

Have you ever thought, "Wouldn't it be wonderful to simply spend time informally with Jesus?" How incredible it must have been for the disciples to watch Him perform miracles, to listen to Him teach, to be able to ask Him questions about all the things they didn't understand. You can imagine, then, the disciples' shock when Jesus told them that they would be better off if He went away. He said, "I tell you the truth, it is to your advantage that I go away; for if I do not go away, the Helper shall not come to you; but if I go, I will send Him to you" (John 16:7). What did Jesus mean?

When Jesus walked the earth in person, with all the limitations of a physical body, He could be in only one place at a time. He could speak to only one person or group at a time, and He could perform His mighty miracles only for those individuals with whom He had immediate contact (although the Bible records a few instances in which Jesus healed someone without the person physically being in His presence).

When the Holy Spirit was poured out on the Day of Pentecost (Acts 2:1–42), Jesus's presence and power filled each of the believers. Now He can be with all of us, all the time, by His Spirit. He can be speaking to you wherever you are right now while at the same time He can be speaking to me. Similarly His supernatural power is available to all of us, twenty-four hours a day, every day.

We can walk with Him, talk with Him, ask Him any question that is on our minds. Furthermore, the same Spirit who inspired the biblical writers to put the Word of God in print now illumines our minds to understand the truths God wants us to know. Jesus told His disciples the night before His death, "But when He, the Spirit of truth, comes, He will guide you into all the truth; for He will not speak on His own initiative, but whatever He hears, He will speak; and He will disclose to you what is to come. He will glorify Me, for He will take of Mine and will disclose it to you. All things that the Father has are Mine; therefore I said that He takes of Mine and will disclose it to you" (John 16:13–15).

The Holy Spirit Has Personality

Notice that Jesus always refers to the Holy Spirit as a person—He or Him, never as an "it." You would never refer to your husband or wife as an "it." You wouldn't say, "Yes, it and I had a marvelous vacation." Yet many Christians do something equally as foolish by referring to the Holy Spirit as though He were some vague, ambiguous spiritual force. The Holy Spirit is a person, a person who cannot usually be beheld with the physical senses but a person nonetheless.

He can speak (Acts 13:2); He guides us to the truth (John 16:13); He understands and can communicate (1 Cor. 2:9–12). The Holy Spirit can be resisted (Acts 7:51), grieved (Eph. 4:30), or insulted (Heb. 10:29).

He teaches us what Jesus wants us to know (John 14:26; 16:7–15); He helps us to know Christ better (1 Cor. 2:1–13); He helps us to think as Jesus does, giving us Christlike attitudes (1 Cor. 2:16); He helps us to avoid sin and to do what is right (1 Cor.

6:11); He convicts us of sin and shows us the truth about God's justice and judgment (John 16:8).

Most important of all, the Holy Spirit always glorifies Jesus (John 16:14). The Holy Spirit never attracts the attention to Himself; He always points to Jesus Christ. Certainly we should honor the Holy Spirit in our churches and in our lives, but we should take care not to exalt the Spirit above Jesus. The Holy Spirit always exalts Christ.

God wants to fill your life with the Holy Spirit (Eph. 5:18). If you will allow Him, He will create in you the character of Jesus. It will still be you—your body, mind, and heart—but in a real way, Jesus will be at the center of your life. He will be in charge. The Holy Spirit will give you the inner power to be like Jesus, to be His witness in the world and to overcome the evil one, Satan. When you are filled with the Holy Spirit, then you will begin to understand what the apostle Paul called "the mystery which has been hidden from the past ages and generations, but has now been manifested to His saints…which is Christ in you, the hope of glory" (Col. 1:26–27).

WHY YOU NEED THE POWER OF THE SPIRIT

Probably dozens of reasons could be listed to explain why we need to be filled with the Holy Spirit. Three reasons stand out: the deep-rooted nature of sin, the impossibility of the task Jesus has given us, and the accusations of Satan.

1. The deep-rooted nature of sin

Have you discovered that you are still attracted to sin, even though you are a Christian? If you haven't encountered that shocking revelation yet, you will. Something sinful remains in our hearts even after believing on Jesus, something that causes us to want to do wrong rather than right. The apostle Paul expressed it well for all of us when he said:

> I don't understand myself at all, for I really want to do what is right, but I can't. I do what I don't want to—what I hate. I know perfectly well that what I am doing is wrong, and my bad conscience proves that I agree with these laws I am breaking. But I can't help myself, because I'm no longer doing it. It is sin inside me that is stronger than I am that makes me do these evil things.
>
> I know I am rotten through and through so far as my old sinful nature is concerned. No matter which way I turn I can't make myself do right. I want to but I can't. When I want to do good, I don't; and when I try not to do wrong, I do it anyway. Now if I am doing what I don't want to, it is plain where the trouble is: sin still has me in its evil grasp.
>
> —ROMANS 7:15–20, TLB

Have you ever felt like that? Most of us have. At some point after you have fallen in love with Jesus and committed yourself to Him, you discover, to your horror, that you are totally unable to live the way He wants you to live. You're not alone. Nearly every man and woman who has made a significant impact upon the world for Christ's sake came to a point in his or her life when he or she said, "Wait a minute! My Christian life isn't working. I want to live like Jesus, but I can't do it. I keep getting tripped up by sin."

As a young boy I loved to play baseball in our backyard. The only problem was we had too many trees dotting the landscape. My dad and I chopped down several of the trees that blocked our base paths, but we weren't able to remove the tree stumps or the roots. As a result, every once in a while a runner would be rounding second or third base and would get tripped up by one of those remaining stumps or roots. *Splaaat!* He'd fall right on his face.

Finally an old farmer who was watching us play said, "Son, if you don't get those stumps and roots out of there, somebody's gonna get hurt."

"Yes, sir, I know that," I answered, "but we've tried to chop them as low as we can get them. We can't get a saw or an ax any lower."

"Hmmph," the old man grunted. "Only one thing will get stumps and roots like that out of the ground."

"Oh, really? What's that?"

"Dynamite!"

He was right. If you visit our former home today, the stumps and roots are gone.

In Acts 1:8 just before Jesus ascended into heaven, He told His disciples, "But you will receive power when the Holy Spirit has come upon you; and you shall be My witnesses both in Jerusalem, and in all Judea and Samaria, and even to the remotest part of the earth." The word Jesus used for power is *dunamis*; it is the same root from which we derive our words *dynamite*, *dynamic*, and *dynamo*.

God wants to apply the dynamite power of His Holy Spirit to the sin and its roots that run deeply into your heart. Better yet, He not only wants to radically deal with those roots, He also wants to give you the power to reject the desire for evil things and give you a desire for holy, righteous things. As Paul said, "Sin shall not be master over you" (Rom. 6:14). God wants to clean out your subconscious mind, that area in which you have been tamping down hurt and bitterness, awful memories, failures, and painful past experiences. And the good news is, the Holy Spirit is powerful enough to do it.

At the conclusion of Paul's lament in Romans 7, he cries out, "Wretched man that I am! Who will set me free from the body of this death?" (v. 24). He suddenly sees the light and says, "Thanks be to God through Jesus Christ our Lord!" (v. 25). Then in Romans 8 Paul immediately launches into a discussion of the Spirit-led life, mentioning the Holy Spirit fifteen times. The difference between Romans 7 and Romans 8 is astounding. In Romans 7 the emphasis is on "I," me at my best, still an abject failure in my Christian life and a slave to sin. In Romans 8 the Holy Spirit is in charge, and the first verse trumpets the change: "Therefore there is now no condemnation for those who are in Christ Jesus." The stumps and roots of sin have been overcome by the power of the Holy Spirit.

2. The impossibility of the task

A second reason you need to be filled with the Holy Spirit is the impossibility of the task Jesus has assigned to you. Do you realize what Jesus has called you to do? He has commanded you to take the gospel to the entire world (Matt. 28:18–20; Mark 16:15–16)! The Great Commission does not apply only to missionaries in a foreign land or other "superspiritual saints." It is a direct command to you and me as well. All of us are called to be involved somehow in taking Christ's message to the world.

But if you are like most people, you are probably having trouble taking the gospel down the street to your coworkers or family members. Precisely at this point the Holy Spirit wants to empower your witness. Jesus said that after the Holy Spirit comes upon us, we will be His witnesses (Acts 1:8). Notice He didn't say you would simply talk about Him. He said you would be His witness—in every area of your life, in everything you do, in your personal demeanor, in the way you act in church as well as the way you conduct yourself in the mall, on a ball field, or dance floor. When the Holy Spirit fills up your life, everything about you will point people to Jesus. Oh, yes, occasionally you may even open your mouth and talk about Him!

Without the Holy Spirit's presence, there will be little power in your actions or words when you attempt to introduce people to Jesus or when you endeavor to engage the enemy in spiritual warfare. No doubt that is one reason Jesus instructed His disciples to return to Jerusalem and wait for the power of the Holy Spirit to come upon them before they went out to represent Him to the world or before trying to take authority over any evil spirits.

Jesus knew the job He wanted His disciples to do was too big for them to attempt on their own power. The world then, as it is now, was largely unreceptive and antagonistic to the message of Jesus. Even though His disciples were eyewitnesses to the risen Christ, Jesus knew if they were to have an eternal impact and to change the course of human history, they must be filled with the Holy Spirit. Just before He ascended to heaven, He told His disciples, "And behold, I am sending forth the promise of My Father upon you; but you are to stay in the city until you are clothed with power from on high" (Luke 24:49).

The disciples obeyed Jesus's instructions, and on the Day of Pentecost the Holy Spirit was poured out upon them (Acts 2). They were a small group at first, only one hundred twenty believers who gathered in an upper room in Jerusalem. Most of the people there were poor in financial terms; many of them were uneducated; none of them were trained witnesses or counselors; few, if any, were professional politicians, social strategists, or powerful orators. But they waited for the power of the Holy Spirit, and they received His presence in a powerful way. They went out with His supernatural anointing and literally changed their world by the power of God. After the believers were filled with the Holy Spirit, three thousand people came to know Jesus in one day (v. 41). "And the Lord was adding to their number day by day those who were being saved" (v. 47).

Wherever the Lord finds a person with a willing heart, God is still pouring out His Holy Spirit today. Jeff was lamenting the lack of enthusiasm in his church. "I just don't get anything out of it," he said sincerely. "Our church is boring."

"Well, what are you putting into it?" I asked him. It was a direct question. I hadn't intended it to be piercing or probing; I was simply seeking information so I could encourage Jeff. But the Spirit of God used my words to speak to Jeff's heart.

"Yes," he said, as though somebody had turned on a light in his mind. "I guess I really haven't been putting much effort into trying to make things better. Hey, thanks a lot." And he was gone.

"Any time," I answered as I watched him go.

Jeff went back to his church and threw himself into getting involved. He enjoyed meeting new people and helping the group's energy rise, but he was still not having a significant spiritual impact. Then one night after a church service, a group of Jeff's friends gathered around him, laid their hands upon his shoulders and head, and prayed for Jeff to be filled with the Holy Spirit. Jeff prayed as well. He said, "God, I've been a Christian ever since I can remember, but something is missing. I give myself completely to You. Please come and fill me with Your Spirit."

As the group continued to pray, suddenly the Holy Spirit swept through their midst. Instinctively Jeff fell to his knees and bowed his head. Others in the group did the same. The Holy Spirit filled Jeff's life and several others who were praying with the group. Still on their knees, they raised their faces upward and began to worship the Lord Jesus. They laughed; they sang; they prayed some more; mostly they praised the name of Jesus.

It was an exhilarating experience, but everyone including Jeff wondered if they would revert to life as usual. They didn't. With Jeff leading the way, they began telling everyone they met about Jesus. Other people who had been on the fringes of their church came to know Jesus as a result. Many others were convicted of their own complacency as they observed their friends getting "on fire" by the power of the Holy Spirit.

The church continued to grow, and the impact spilled over into the community. High school students began carrying their Bibles to school; adults looked for opportunities to talk about the Lord at every juncture. And dozens of people were introduced to Jesus each week.

Additionally these Spirit-empowered believers began praying against the devil's influence in their town, taking authority over certain evil spirits that had a hold on the local school system. The high school had been shaken by several suicides among the student body, so the Spirit-filled Christians began praying against the "spirit of suicide." The school also had more than its share of premarital pregnancies, so the Christians began to pray against a "spirit of unbridled lust" that they felt had permeated the student body. They prayed that lust's power would be broken and a new spirit of sexual purity would be established. Within a few months the school board instituted two programs, one to help build students' self-esteem and the other to encourage sexual abstinence as a way to prevent premarital pregnancies and sexually transmitted diseases.

Jeff and other members of their church are continuing to have a powerful impact on the fabric of their community. When I saw Jeff last, he quipped, "I'll tell you one thing—church isn't boring anymore!"

3. The accusations of Satan

The third reason you need to be filled with the Holy Spirit is because that is the only safe way of overcoming the accusations of Satan. The devil is a formidable foe. He is smart; he is deceitful; and, remember, his goals are to rob, kill, and destroy you.

The Bible also refers to the devil as "the accuser of our brethren" (Rev. 12:10) and says he accuses us before our God day and night. The devil is like a troublemaker at school who teases, coaxes, and cajoles you into doing something wrong, and then when you do it, he immediately squeals to the teacher. Satan does his worst in tempting you to sin, and then as soon as you do he throws it back in your face. Not only that, but he also accuses you before God. Satan says, "God, did you see what he (or she) did? And he's supposed to be a Christian? One of your children? Ha!"

ACCUSATION VS. CONVICTION

Satan especially loves to rant and rail about your past failures. He says, "See, you're never going to get it together with God. You keep falling backward. Don't you remember that awful sin you committed last month? Do you really think God is going to forgive you for that and let it go? No way! You're going to have to pay." What's going on here? Is Satan attempting to help the Holy Spirit in your life? Not a chance. Satan heaps accusations upon you to condemn you and to encourage you to condemn yourself.

The Holy Spirit does not convict you to condemn you, nor does He accuse you. He will convict you of sin, righteousness, and judgment (John 16:8) so you can repent of your sin and get clean. But once you have repented and received God's forgiveness, He will never again mention that sin to you, not even on judgment day. God will not say to you, "Remember that sin you committed back there in 1997?" No, that sin is gone. If you have sought God's forgiveness, the blood of Jesus has cleansed that sin. God Himself has chosen to forget that sin ever happened.

You need to recognize the difference between Satan's accusations and the Holy Spirit's conviction. How can you tell the difference? Easy. If you are feeling guilty and shameful for a sin of which you know you have been forgiven, that is Satan attempting to accuse you and to heap more abuse upon you. Tell Satan off. Say to him, "Look, you devil, that sin has been washed away by the blood of Jesus, and you have no right to resurrect it."

There's another way you can discern between accusation and conviction: if your awareness of sin is driving you away from God in bitterness and resentment rather than causing you to seek Him with a repentant heart, then you know you are being victimized by a satanic accusation. Remember, it is Satan who tries to use sin against you, not God. The Holy Spirit wants you to find freedom from your sin; He does not want to use it as a club.

Satan is a master of reverse psychology in this regard. To some people he says, "You are not such a bad person, especially compared to other people. Look at them. They are the ones who need to repent, not you. Your sin is infinitesimal compared with theirs. Someday you may want to repent, when you accumulate a stack of serious sins. But not now. Later. Don't bother God about your measly little sin."

With others Satan reverses his tack and says, "Your sin is too awful. God could never forgive you. After all you have done? Don't even think about trying to get it together with God."

Both tactics are sinister lies. God hates sin. Period. Big sins, little sins, horrible, ghastly sins, or "little white lies." God hates them all because they separate you from Him and, if they are not cleansed, hold the potential to plunge you into hell. On the other hand, all sin except blasphemy of the Holy Spirit is forgivable.

Blasphemy of the Holy Spirit (Matt. 12:24–32) is not merely saying or doing nasty things against God's Spirit. It may mean that a person can become so spiritually insensitive, so hard-hearted, that he or she cannot even discern the Holy Spirit's convicting voice any longer. When a person cannot or will not be convicted of sin, it is impossible to repent and return to a right relationship with God.

More likely, the unpardonable sin is attributing the work of the Holy Spirit to the devil. This was the sin many of the Jewish leaders committed in Jesus's time. They not only opposed Jesus; they also accused Him of performing miracles by the power of Satan. They were so consumed with their own sinfulness, they rejected Jesus and what the Holy Spirit in Him was doing right in front of them.

The Bible says, "The blood of Jesus His Son cleanses us from all sin" (1 John 1:7). Don't allow the devil to dupe you into believing that you have irreparably destroyed your relationship with God. If you are even remotely sensitive to the Holy Spirit's voice speaking to your heart and mind, you can be assured that God hasn't given up on you.

When You Repent, He Restores

The devil likes to beat you over the head with feelings of unworthiness, insecurity, and doubt. But the Holy Spirit always comes as a "gentleman," in a gentle sort of way. Not that he isn't direct and to the point when dealing with sin. He is. But His approach is always designed to bring you to repentance and restoration rather than to send you running for the hills.

Here's how the Holy Spirit usually works: the moment you say or do something wrong, the Spirit of God speaks to your heart, mind, and conscience. He says something like, "Those words you spoke may have been correct, but your attitude was wrong." Or he may say, "What you did was right, but your motive for doing it was absolutely selfish."

At that point you have a decision to make. You can either repent of your wrong attitude and motives, or you can pretend you didn't notice the Holy Spirit speaking to you or that you didn't understand what He meant. The Spirit is never pushy, but when you try to fake Him out, He comes right back with a powerful dose of conviction and usually gets even more specific.

"You said *that* to this person and your words were unnecessarily harsh. You offended that person, and you have offended God. You need to repent and make it right."

Again you have a choice. The Holy Spirit will not force you to do something you are unwilling to do. He speaks gently but firmly, showing you your sin and what you need to do about it. The next step of obedience is up to you. If you choose to ignore the Spirit's voice, you become more calloused in your spirit. You will sense yourself stepping out of God's will for your life, slipping backward instead of moving forward in obedience to His Spirit.

The Holy Spirit will continue to speak to you about the matter. In fact, you will not be able to progress further with God until you deal with the sin. But if you continue to harden your heart and resist the Holy Spirit, you step out from under the Lord's protective "umbrella" and open the door to the devil's fiery darts. And guess where those darts hit? In the exact area about which the Holy Spirit has been speaking to you. For the sake of your relationship with God and your own good, learn to repent of any sin as soon as the Holy Spirit convicts you of it. God will forgive and restore you to a right relationship with Him and give you the courage to seek reconciliation with the person you offended.

Nobody who knows better will ever say that Christians never sin. The key to successful Christian living, however, is to keep "short accounts" with God. When you sin, repent as soon as the Spirit brings the slip-up to your attention. Do not give the devil any further opportunity to use that failure or infraction of God's Word against you.

The devil does not always launch a barrage of randomly sent missiles. When he or his demons discover an area of disobedience to the Holy Spirit in your life, the devil launches a series of "homing" missiles, "smart bombs" zooming in on the unprotected area, scoring direct hits, and inflicting as much pain as possible.

That is why you need to be filled with the Holy Spirit afresh each day, to overcome temptation and to shut the door to satanic attacks. It's your choice, the devil or the dove (the symbol for the Holy Spirit). Whatever you do, please don't try to overpower the devil or his demons if you are not filled with the Holy Spirit. The devil has been in business a long time. He knows how to detect any area of weakness, carnality (fleshly lusts stemming from self-interest), or compromise in you, and he will be quick to use whatever he can against you. But when you are filled with the Spirit of Jesus and daily put on the armor of God and resist the devil, Satan will flee from you (James 4:7).

CAN A CHRISTIAN HAVE A DEMON?

Bible scholars differ drastically in their opinions concerning whether or not, or to what degree, a Christian can be demonized. I do not believe that an evil spirit can *possess* a born-again, Spirit-filled Christian. Frankly I've seen very few unbelievers who I felt were possessed by demons, if by the term "demon possession," we mean, "completely and continuously controlled by demons."

On the other hand, I have encountered many individuals, both Christian and non-Christian, who are being *oppressed* by demons. Particular areas of their lives seem unusually susceptible to temptation or other demonic activity. Sincere Christians who are being oppressed by demons will sometimes do things that go against everything they believe, and yet the individuals feel powerless to resist these evils. Why is this?

The cause can usually be traced to two reasons, one being the flipside of the other. First, Satan has gained a foothold in their lives somehow, most likely through the effects of sin—their

184

own sin or someone else's sin committed against them. Second, they were not filled with the Holy Spirit; some area of their life was exposed because it was not surrendered to Christ, and the devil's emissaries came knocking on that unprotected entrance. At first they may have resisted the devil's deceptions and enticements through sheer willpower. But before long they found themselves slipping in their spiritual lives while at the same time opening the door wider to demonic influences.

Any area that is not filled by the Holy Spirit and under His control is a wide-open target for satanic oppression. To be safe from the devil's attacks, everything about you must be brought under Christ's Lordship and submitted to His control, including your family, career, social life, money, car, clothing, relationships, attitudes, and goals. Everything. You must be filled with the Holy Spirit if you are going to live in freedom. How can you do that? Let's see.

Chapter Sixteen

HOW TO BE FILLED WITH THE HOLY SPIRIT

I'VE OFTEN WONDERED if the apostle Paul was a golfer. His description in Romans 7 sounds much like my golf game: "The shots I want to hit, I don't, and the shots I don't want to hit are the ones I do." At least Paul could blame Satan for his spiritual frustration; I can't blame anybody but me for my poor golf game.

But I am consistent. I invariably score in the nineties—sometimes for the first nine holes! I played so poorly in one tournament, the sponsors gave me an award: for being the absolute worst golfer on the course that day. I think the club management figured that if they humiliated me badly enough, I wouldn't return to their course, but I fooled them. Like a glutton for punishment, I kept going back. After all, I hold some dubious distinctions at that course. For example, who else do you know who could hit a golf ball down the fairway and actually *lose* yardage? (I don't know why they ever put that rock in the middle of the golf course, anyhow.)

But suppose that to please God and get into heaven, I have to be a good golfer and par every hole on the course. Guess who is in big trouble?

Oh, sure, I'd be out there trying, swinging away for all I am worth. But it would be the same old story—hooks, slices, and *ker-plunks* (the balls I hit in the ponds, giving new meaning to the scripture, "All have sinned and fallen short...").

Now imagine that some genius came up with a serum that could be injected into me and give me the ability to play par golf. I could be a great golfer if I agree to just two conditions: (1) that I admit I am a lousy golfer (as part of that confession, I may have some divots or ball marks to go back and repair); (2) that I willfully submit to the injection.

What do you think I would do? You betcha! I'd say, "Give me that super serum. I'm tired of always falling short, even when I have given it my best shot. I need something to change my very nature and make me into the kind of golfer I ought to be."

Please forgive my foolish illustration, but something like that actually happens (though it has nothing to do with golf) when the Holy Spirit comes and fills your life. He gives you the power *within* so you can live the way God commands. It is no longer your ability that matters, only your availability, your willingness to allow Him to work in and through you. Being filled with the Holy Spirit is not something you do for God. It is something He does for you! What, then, is required for you to receive His gift?

BELIEVE THAT GOD CAN FILL YOU

God wants to fill you with His Spirit, and He has promised that He will, if you will trust Him. Jesus said, "If you then, being evil, know how to give good gifts to your children, how much more will your heavenly Father give the Holy Spirit to those who ask Him?" (Luke 11:13).

On the Day of Pentecost, when the Holy Spirit was poured out on the disciples and many others, Peter told a crowd of people, "Repent, and each of you be baptized in the name of Jesus Christ for the forgiveness of your sins; and you will receive the gift of the Holy Spirit. For the promise is for you and your children and for all who are far off, as many as the Lord our God will call to Himself" (Acts 2:38–39).

Not only is the infilling of the Holy Spirit a promise of God, but it is also a clear command of God. Paul wrote in Ephesians 5:18, "And do not get drunk with wine, for that is dissipation, but be filled with the Spirit."

Paul's contrast between being drunk and being filled with the Holy Spirit may strike you as strange, but when you stop to think about it, the contrast makes sense. Have you ever seen a person who was inebriated in only one part of his or her body? Of course not. If a person is drunk, every part of his or her body and personality is affected by the "spirits." Similarly the Holy Spirit fills and affects every area of your life.

The Spirit-filled life is not optional equipment for a Christian. Nor is the fullness of the Spirit merely a goal to be sought after but never attained in this life. When God gives you a promise and a command, you can be certain that it is important and possible.

Many Christians hedge, "Yes, I know I ought to be filled with the Holy Spirit, but I am not. I know I need to be filled because the devil is beating me up one end and down the other, but I'm just not ready." With an attitude like that, they may never be ready!

John Wesley, the founder of the Methodist Church, often asked his audiences penetrating questions similar to these:

- Have you received the Holy Spirit's fullness since you believed?

- Will you ever need Him more than you do right now?

- Will you ever be "more ready" to receive Him than right now?

- Will God ever be "more ready" to fill you with
His Holy Spirit than He is right now?

If you answered no to any of the above questions, then begin to believe right now that God wants to fill you with an overflowing portion of His Holy Spirit. Tell the Lord that you are willing to receive all He wants to give you.

RENOUNCE ALL SIN

If you have been dabbling with demonic practices such as Ouija boards, tarot cards, television psychics, witchcraft (or Wiccan), black magic, fortune-tellers, New Age religions, or any cultist practices, repent and renounce those things right now. To repent means to turn around one hundred eighty degrees—not partially but completely turning away from your past sinful practices. Ask God to forgive you for worshipping these false gods; then renounce any sinful associations or demonic strongholds in your life. Speak aloud and say something such as, "I cast off this thing, and I don't want it in my life any longer. I refuse to serve it any more. From this day forth I will serve only one Lord, the Lord Jesus Christ."

Confess any known sin to the Lord and ask Him to give you a clean heart. This step is crucial, because if the Holy Spirit is revealing an area of sin in your life and you refuse to repent of it, your spiritual progress will stall at that point until you are willing to allow Him to cleanse you. If you aren't sure which sin, if any, is blocking the flow of His Spirit in your life, pray something similar to this: "Lord, please convict me of my sinfulness." Then watch out! It may be the fastest response to prayer you've ever received.

Are you reluctant to give up your sin? Risk it. Frankly you can always return to your filth if you find you are not satisfied with Jesus. The devil will always be glad to take you back. On the other hand, once you experience the power of God's Spirit working in and through you, sin, no matter how tasty or tantalizing, will never satisfy you again.

As a little boy my favorite playgrounds were the mounds of black, bituminous coal slag that rose all around our Pennsylvania town. After a delightful day in the coal dust, I'd trudge home, deviously trying to devise some way to avoid taking a bath. I was filthy and proud of it! Normally my parents had to beg, threaten, or trick me into the tub.

Then one day I discovered girls. Suddenly, being clean seemed so exciting! I never wanted to be dirty again. Something similar happens when you discover how beautiful a Spirit-filled life can be. Sin will lose its fatal attraction.

HOLD NOTHING BACK

Surrender completely every area of your life to the control of Christ. This is no time for hypocrisy. You can't bargain with God ("I'll give You this area, God, if You will give me that gift"). Simply obey Christ and allow Him to have absolute control of your life. As you do, He will fill you with His Spirit. He will then continue the process, producing more and more of His character—the fruit of the Spirit—in you.

This is a never-ending process, known as sanctification, and it will continue as long as you live. You will never exhaust God's fresh supply of resources in your life. Maybe that's why Spirit-filled Christians rarely become bored. Just about the time you say, "OK, Lord, I think I have a handle on this Christian life. I think I've gone as far as I can go," He says, "Oh, really? Well, open wide, because I'm going to do something even more incredible in your heart, something your mind hasn't yet imagined." What an exciting way to live! And it begins the moment you wholeheartedly place your life in the Lord's hands.

William Booth, the founder of The Salvation Army, was

often asked the secret to his spiritual success. In his later years the great general would respond, "The secret of my success is that God had all there was of William Booth."[1] That will be the secret of your success and mine as well.

TRUST AND OBEY

Trust the Lord with childlike faith to be faithful to His Word. This is His promise we are talking about, His command that you be filled with the Holy Spirit. As the apostle Paul prayed for the new Christians at Thessalonica to be filled with the Spirit, he reminded them, "Faithful is He who calls you, and He also will bring it to pass" (1 Thess. 5:24). You needn't try to conjure up some experience that you heard happened to somebody else, nor do you need to fake the gifts of the Spirit or the fruit of the Spirit. Allow Jesus to bring about the results of His Spirit in your life. Your job is just to graciously accept all that Jesus has for you and to use all He gives you for His glory.

THE NEW YOU

As you cooperate with the Holy Spirit in the reprogramming of your life, not only will you have a new power, but you will also sense a new purity, a new (or renewed) purpose in life, and a peace in your heart and mind unlike anything the world has to offer (John 14:27).

Furthermore you will notice the Bible becoming an exciting book to you. The same Spirit who inspired the Word of God will illuminate the Scriptures in your mind. Moreover, prayer will take on a new dimension for you. It will cease to be a "Christmas list" with an *Amen* tacked on the end of it. Your prayer time will become genuine communication with your Creator. In addition, as you see the Spirit of Christ working in and through your personality, you will sense a new capacity and desire to praise the Lord Jesus, to worship Him, and to tell other people of what

He has done in your life. You will become a testimony of His greatness.

Paul talked about the Spirit's radical transformation of our lives in this way: "That, in reference to your former manner of life, you lay aside the old self, which is being corrupted in accordance with the lusts of deceit, and that you be renewed in the spirit of your mind, and put on the new self, which in the likeness of God has been created in righteousness and holiness of the truth" (Eph. 4:22–24).

In the passage that follows (Eph. 4:25–6:20), Paul presents one of the best discussions of practical Christianity in the Bible. In this wonderfully down-to-earth material, two highlights stand out that seem to be Paul's overriding themes: (1) "do not give the devil an opportunity" (Eph. 4:27), and (2) "do not grieve the Holy Spirit of God" (v. 30).

Intriguing, isn't it, that Paul should feel the need to emphasize these two principles to Spirit-filled believers? Yet God is impressing that same message on us today. Some of the old-time saints used to talk about this in terms of overcoming the world, the flesh, and the devil (Eph. 2:1–3). Let's take a practical look at what that means.

Chapter Seventeen

HOOKS FROM HELL

IN A SCENE from the Steven Spielberg movie *Hook*, the villain, Captain James Hook, and his bumbling assistant, Smee, are trying to come up with a way to get even with Peter Pan for defeating Hook long ago and indirectly causing Hook's hand to be bitten off by a crocodile.

Suddenly Smee has an idea: "Pan's kids..." he says intently to Captain Hook. "You could make them like you.... You could make the little buggers love you!"

Hook answers sardonically, "No, Smee, no little children love me."

"Captain, that is the point," Smee squeals. "That is the ultimate revenge.... Pan's kids in love with Hook.... It's the ultimate payback."

Hook begins to see the possibilities and croons, "You know, Smee, I like it. Oh, Smee, what a superb idea I just had. Tomorrow I will make Pan's brats love me!"[1] And he does. He sets about luring Pan's kids away from their father. Hook caters to every desire Pan's kids can imagine, spoiling them rotten like himself. He would have ultimately destroyed them had Peter Pan not come to their rescue.

Since the days of Adam and Eve the devil has been using a ploy similar to Captain Hook's. Satan has been trying to get even with God for quelling his rebellion and casting him out of heaven along with one-third of heaven's angels. But Satan's schemes and revenge have been grossly unsuccessful. He failed to keep Jesus from being born, he failed to kill Jesus as a baby, he failed in his efforts to distract Jesus from His mission, and he failed big-time when Jesus died on the cross, purchasing our salvation. The ultimate insult to Satan (but by no means the last) was when all of his demonic cohorts failed to keep Jesus in the grave. Satan could only sit by as a spectator when Jesus Christ rose victoriously over death, the grave, and hell itself.

The one way Satan has succeeded in striking at God's heart has been through His "kids," using every possible method to keep them out of the kingdom. For years Satan has bludgeoned, bruised, and persecuted Christians, killing off as many as he could. Now in these days the devil has taken a different tack. He is luring many of God's kids away from their heavenly Father by giving them anything and everything they want. You might call his strategy "saturation sin."

We know the Lord Jesus will return soon to rescue His "kids," and the "Hook from hell" will finally be defeated. Until that time, however, Satan is hooking the hearts of many people through ancient temptations wrapped in new packages, sugar-coated and garnished with new accessibility and acceptability.

Sexual Sins

You would have to be a recent drop-in from planet Zulu not to know that we are living in an R-rated society. Premarital sex, extramarital sex, multiple partners, kinky sex, any and every kind of sex is readily available. Pornography abounds. Television programs and movies are increasingly explicit in their presentations of erotic material. Homosexuality is advocated as a "normal lifestyle," demanding public acceptance and the full privileges of heterosexual marriage. Incidents of rape, premarital pregnancies, and abortions continue unabated in our "civilized" society, but the soaring statistics roll off our numbed senses.

Consequently even sincere Christians are questioning biblical codes of morality. Because Satan uses our God-given sexuality against us in so many ways, a brief review of God's standards may be helpful. First, God always speaks favorably about the sexual relationship within the context of marriage. God is not opposed to sex, but He is adamantly opposed to the misuse of sex. He Word says, "Marriage is to be held in honor among all, and the marriage bed is to be undefiled; for fornicators and adulterers God will judge" (Heb. 13:4).

Clearly the Bible condemns all sex outside the bonds of marriage. It labels all such conduct as sin and warns that God will pour out His wrath upon fornicators (those who engage in premarital sex) and adulterers (those who sexually compromise the marriage commitment). In case we were still wondering about God's will in this matter, His Word says: "Do not be deceived; nether fornicators, nor idolaters, nor adulterers, nor effeminate, nor homosexuals...will inherit the kingdom of God" (1 Cor. 6:9–10).

Don't be deceived by what you hear on the talk-show circuits, on albums, TV, or in the movies. God's standards concerning sex have not changed. His Word says: "For this is the will of God, your sanctification; that is, that you abstain from sexual immorality" (1 Thess. 4:3). Not much wiggle room, is there?

Why does God give us such strict rules regarding our sexuality? Simple. The sexual relationship between a man and a woman is a symbol of the intimacy God intends to have with His people. Throughout the Bible, when God's people were unfaithful to Him, they were denounced as adulterers. There is a holiness about sex that we scarcely understand.

Moreover, God wants you to enjoy your sexuality and to have a super sex life—at the right time and with the person to whom you are married. God knows that all other kinds of sexual relations are always destructive, so He has given us regulations governing our sexuality for our own good—so we won't hurt ourselves, and so we don't harm others.

Furthermore, when a person tastes the forbidden fruit of sexual immorality, he or she becomes a prime target for demonic activity. Something about your sexuality is so sacred and intimate that the devil knows that if he can get you to compromise sexually, he has *you*.

No Excuses

Understand, while we understand the temptations and should always express compassion and encouragement for those who have committed sexual sins in the past or are struggling to avoid sexual sins in the present, we dare not make excuses for sexual immorality. God's Word tells us that each of us is responsible for our own actions and cautions "that each of you know how to possess his own vessel in sanctification and honor, not in lustful passion, like the Gentiles who do not know God" (1 Thess. 4:4–5). Nevertheless, it cannot be denied that some people, including Christians, are so bound by sexual obsessions, they seem unable or unwilling to help themselves.

How does this happen? One thing is certain: temptation is not from God. The Bible states clearly: "Let no one say when he is tempted, 'I am being tempted by God'; for God cannot be tempted by evil, and He Himself does not tempt anyone. But each one is tempted when he is carried away and enticed by his own lust. Then when lust has conceived, it gives birth to sin; and when sin is accomplished, it brings forth death" (James 1:13–15).

The downhill slide begins in the mind, when a person dwells on impure thoughts. The thoughts lead to a series of wrong choices and unwise actions. The Holy Spirit convicts the person of his or her mental fantasies and immoral activities, but if the individual refuses to repent of these sins and take steps to change the mental input or stimulation, the actions soon become habitual. More and more the person has less and less control. At this point if demonic activity is part of the problem, it is highly unlikely that the person will be unable to free himself or herself from sexual sin.

The good news is, any demonic power or patterns can be broken by the power of Jesus Christ. If you are in bondage to sexual immorality, you may or may not want to seek outside help from your pastor or a professional counselor, but be assured, you can get free—if you are willing.

Ordinarily sexual obsessions can be broken through honest repenting and renouncing of any demonic control in your life. As the blood of Jesus cleanses you from all sin, allow His Holy Spirit to come and fill your life. This is crucial. The reason many Christians keep returning to sinful habits after they have confessed and repented is they allow themselves to remain in a spiritual vacuum. The "junk has been cleaned out," but they have not allowed the Holy Spirit to fill that void.

Once, Jesus was rebuking the Pharisees for their insatiable desire for spiritual signs. In doing so, Jesus used a graphic illustration that is typical of many Christians who honestly repent of their sins but are never filled with the Holy Spirit. Jesus said:

> Now when the unclean spirit goes out of a man, it passes through waterless places seeking rest, and does not find it. Then it says, "I will return to my house from which I came"; and when it comes, it finds it unoccupied, swept, and put in order.
>
> Then it goes and takes along with it seven other spirits more wicked than itself, and they go in and live there; and the last state of that man becomes worse than the first.
>
> —MATTHEW 12:43–45

If you are repenting of sexual sins, don't stop short. Allow Jesus to cleanse your heart, mind, and body and restore to you a "spiritual virginity" by which you are as pure as if you had never sinned. Then go on: allow Him to have full control of your life, including your sexuality. Take authority over the devil in Jesus's name and declare your freedom from sexual bondage.

DRINKING, DRUGS, AND THE DEMONIC

Alcohol; destructive, mind-altering drugs; and the demonic almost always seem to piggyback one another, and many men and women have collapsed physically, mentally, and spiritually under these evil influences. Abusive use of alcoholic beverages and drugs have been problems since men and women first discovered that bees were not the only ones in God's creation that could "buzz."

First, let's be honest. The Bible does not say that drinking a glass of wine, beer, or a mixed drink is a sin. It does say that it is wrong for a Christian to get drunk. Nowadays many people want to minimize that truth, but being drunk is listed right along with other major sins in the New Testament (Eph. 5:18; Rom. 13:13; 1 Cor. 6:9–10; Gal. 5:19–21; 1 Pet. 4:3). Paul also taught that Christian leaders should not be inebriated (1 Tim. 3:3; Titus 1:7).

Beyond that, in a discussion of Christian liberty and whether or not the early Christians should eat meat or drink wine that had been sacrificed to idols, Paul saw the possibility of demonic attachment to these items: "What do I mean then? That a thing sacrificed to idols is anything, or that an idol is anything? No, but I say that the things which the Gentiles sacrifice, they sacrifice to demons and not to God; and I do not want you to become sharers in demons. You cannot drink the cup of the Lord and the cup of demons (1 Cor. 10:19–21).

Who needs alcohol, anyhow? To some people, such a question

200

smacks of self-righteousness, but it is not intended to imply any more than a question such as, "Who needs sugar, anyhow?" It is a valid question and worth considering.

"Why do I want to drink alcohol, anyhow?" you should ask. Honest answers, now. After all, most people don't particularly like beer or whiskey the first few times they try them (the same may not be true for tropical mixed drinks). They have to convince themselves to enjoy the taste. But they still drink it. Why? Some people drink to relax or to temporarily escape reality; others drink to consciously or subconsciously lower their inhibitions; many drink to be accepted by their friends, colleagues, or peers.

The truth is, many who feel they need a drink to deal with their problems or to be accepted by others are either immature or mentally ill. Often they are insecure and have a poor self-image. They think that by drinking they can escape themselves for a while and be less fearful, shy, or backward. When they drink, they sometimes say and do things they would not otherwise say or do.

"What's wrong with that?" you may ask. Nothing, except that God wants you to find your freedom through Christ. You don't need a drink or a drug to do that. Jesus wants you to feel better about yourself naturally as a result of knowing Him.

Most Christians are aware of alcohol's dangers. We know that every year thousands of people die in alcohol-related traffic accidents. We understand that alcohol is a leading contributor to or cause of divorce, rape, child and spousal abuse, and violent crime. With this in mind, what message do we send when we imbibe?

"Well, drinking doesn't bother me," some people are quick to say. "I don't get drunk." Granted, but unfortunately some of your friends can't stop with one drink. Your example to other people has to be considered in all that you do.

The apostle Paul gave us a good model to follow. He decided not to eat or drink anything that would cause a weaker Christian to sin. He called this "the law of Love." You can find his advice on the subject in Romans 14–15 and 1 Corinthians 8–10.

DRUG DEMONS

In a town near my home several high school students recently held up a convenience story in broad daylight, hoping to get some money with which they could buy more drugs. The robbery turned sour, and one of the crooks took out a gun and shot and killed the teenage woman behind the counter. The killer and the counter-girl, it was later discovered, were boyfriend and girlfriend. Their sad story reminds us again that drug addiction can cause a person to turn against his or her best friends, lover, or family members. No doubt the devil and his demons celebrate every drug-related tragedy since satanic influences are present with almost all illegal drug use.

Everyone knows drugs are dangerous. Why would anyone risk his or her life for a momentary high, a temporary euphoria?

Most people initially take drugs out of curiosity. "I wonder if this will make me feel better? I want to see what this is like." Similar to alcohol, for many people, using drugs is a key to the door leading to acceptance and approval among peers. This is especially true of youthful users.

Although many parents envision some devilish, malicious character lurking in the shadows or hanging around the school, enticing their children with heroin, the truth is, most teens get turned onto drugs by their own friends. Unfortunately drugs are readily available at most schools and teenage hangouts nowadays. You don't have to go to the sleazy part of town to find them. They are all around you. The easy access to drugs makes them all the more tempting.

Drug users come from all walks of life—rich folks, poor folks, bright people, and dolts. All sorts of people get hooked. Of course, hardly anyone ever plans on becoming addicted, yet millions of people do. Some people use drugs, like alcohol, to escape reality. Maybe they are trying to run away, avoid, or block out troubles at home. Sometimes they are running away from their own anger, loneliness, or their perceived meaninglessness of life.

In the movies people who use drugs are often pictured as tough, hard, and mean. Some are. Most people who are involved in drug abuse, however, are insecure and scared within. They may put up a good front. They may look or act tough. Or maybe they attempt to convey a super-cool image. In most cases they are hurting inside. They are haunted by their own fears, guilt, frustrations, and other negative emotions. Many drug users would love to get clean—if they could.

Similar to alcohol use, the most dangerous aspect of drug abuse is that it rips the doors of your heart and mind right off the hinges and leaves you wide open to demonic attack. Why? Because when people are under the influence of alcohol or drugs, they are obviously not under the control of the Holy Spirit, and they are out of control themselves. They have surrendered their wills to the alcohol or drug, and consequently they are an extremely easy mark for demonic attack and inhabitation.

Understand, any time you totally surrender your will to anything or anybody other than Jesus, you become vulnerable to demonic attack. Similarly, if you misuse your body by getting high on alcohol or drugs, you are inviting demons to make themselves at home in your life.

Not surprisingly, counselors are discovering that many people who need deliverance from demonic oppression have a background laced with alcohol or drugs. Moreover, many who become entranced by strange brew frequently find themselves stewing in estranged relationships with friends, family members, and with God. This "Bud" is not for you.

If alcohol abuse or drug addiction have been a part of your past or are a current source of strong temptation to you, it is quite possible that you need to be delivered from a demonic influence. That is not to minimize your personal responsibility. Indeed, as with any other sin or self-destructive temptation, you must take the authority Jesus has given you in His name and declare your freedom. Your deliverance may be immediate, or it may be progressive, a day-to-day process of declaring your freedom from bondage. You didn't get into bondage overnight, and you probably won't get out that way either. But rest assured, our God is able to deliver you.

Keep in mind the devil desires to destroy you through alcohol, drugs, or anything else he can use to rob you and to kill you. But Jesus came that you might have life in its fullest (John 10:10). Real life—not a fake, momentary alcohol or drug-induced "rush." He wants to give you lasting peace. Jesus said, "You shall know the truth, and the truth will make you free" (John 8:32).

CULTS, THE OCCULT, AND THE NEW AGE

For nearly two months the world's media focused attention upon the man they called the "mad messiah from Waco." David Koresh claimed to be Jesus Christ in sinful form. The psychopathic cult leader may, in fact, have been demon possessed. At minimum his behavior and teaching made it apparent that he was demon oppressed. Nevertheless, the cult leader convinced at least eighty of his followers that his interpretations were the only accurate views of Scripture, that he alone held the key to unlocking the secrets of God's Word.

With his twisted theology he also convinced his followers that, as the messiah, he had the right to have as many wives as he wished, even if the women were married to someone else. He alone was allowed to have sex with the women of the cult, since his seed was "divine." Like most cult leaders, Koresh used sex, fear, withholding of food, embarrassment, and intimidation to keep his followers in line. Add to that mix a strong militaristic dose of apocalyptic preaching—that the world is coming to an end soon, and we are the only ones who are right—and you have all the ingredients for a nightmare.

Sadly the nightmare played out in the middle of the day on April 19, 1993, while the world watched in stunned horror as the television cameras recorded the wind-whipped inferno that swept David Koresh and at least seventy-nine of his followers into eternity. Of the charred, crumbling remains that could be identified, investigators discovered that several of the cult members, including a body identified as Koresh, had bullet holes in their heads.[2]

In the surreal reports and investigations that followed at Koresh's "Ranch Apocalypse," the questions were asked repeatedly, "What is a cult, anyhow? And how could seemingly sane people willingly give over their money, their bodies, their children, and, for many, their lives to an obviously mistaken, deranged leader?"

Members of the national media as well as the US Congress listened intently to anyone who had even a hint of an answer. Many likened the Koresh disaster to the religious cult led by Jim Jones in which more than nine hundred people committed mass suicide at the People's Temple compound in Guyana in 1978.[3] The one answer few in the news media or federal authorities wanted to entertain was the possibility of demonic activity in both the Koresh and Jones cults. Yet underlying every cult is a spirit of Antichrist that finds its roots in the heart of Satan himself.

Jesus prophesied that shortly before He returns to earth in His Second Coming the world would see a rise in false prophets. Matthew records Jesus warning His disciples to beware of the false teachers three times during His last major discourse before going to the cross:

> For many will come in My name, saying, "I am the Christ," and will mislead many.
>
> —MATTHEW 24:5

> Many false prophets will arise and will mislead many.
>
> —MATTHEW 24:11

> For false Christs and false prophets will arise and will show great signs and wonders, so as to mislead, if possible, even the elect.
>
> —MATTHEW 24:24

Although false prophets have flourished and fooled large numbers of people into following them ever since the time of Christ, we are seeing an unprecedented proliferation of cults in the world today. Most cults have grown up only within the past two hundred years. We may well be eyewitnesses to the fulfillment of Jesus's prophecy.

Remember, not all cult members look strange. They all don't shave their heads and sell books or flowers in public places. Strangely, many cults do not attract the "down-and-out" as much as the "up-and-out." I've found that many cult members are upper-middle class, white, and relatively young.

Many are quite sincere. They desire to see a better world and are frustrated at society's inability or unwillingness to change. Many cult members have had troubles in their families and often have strong need for approval. Some lean toward a cult because of a recent failure in a relationship or job. All cult members are looking for something spiritual in which they can believe.

Many cults deny that Jesus Christ came in bodily form, lived, died, and rose again. Most cults deny that Jesus is God (as

Colossians 1:15–16 clearly states). Frequently they center around a strong personality such as David Koresh or Jim Jones.

Cults mix in half-truths that sound Christian but are actually departures from the historical Christian faith. Cults deceive many people, especially those who do not study the Bible for themselves.

Cults thrive on ignorance and uncertainly, often attracting Christians who do not know what they believe or why they believe. Also, Christians who are discouraged or dissatisfied with their own churches often are attracted to cults, lured by the love and the life they see displayed by cult members.

SOME EXAMPLES OF CULTS

By the definition above, the following are some of the many groups considered to be cults:

Practicers of Transcendental Meditation (TM). TM is a type of Hindu meditation. It claims to provide inner peace and relief from stress without being a religion.

Yoga. This is a "cousin" to TM. It too is a form of Hinduism. The word *yoga* means *union*, referring to the mythical state of "oneness of all things."

The Unification Church, sometimes called the "Moonies," referring to their leader, Sun Myung Moon. This group often uses other community-oriented names to attract local interest.

Hare Krishnas (The International Society for Krishna Consciousness). You may have seen this strange-looking group dancing and chanting on public streets.

The Children of God or Family of Love. Known for promoting sexual promiscuity. Don't be misled by the lovely names.

The Divine Light Mission. Followers of the Divine Light worship the pudgy, round-faced guru Maharaj Ji. Divine Light is another variant of Hinduism; it asserts that you can find God, or more accurately, "God-realization," only with the help of a guru.

Erhard Seminars Training (EST). Founded by Werner Erhard, EST is basically a religious philosophy that can be summarized as: "What is, is." It emphasizes a renewing of your self-image by stripping away a person's emotional coping mechanisms, then rebuilding them from a selfish center. Whatever is good for you is considered "good," regardless of morality or biblically based ethics.

Rastafarians. Rastas believe that former Ethiopian Emperor Haile Selassie is their messiah. Popularized by reggae musician Bob Marley, many Rastafarians make heavy use of marijuana and other drugs as part of their faith and lifestyle.

Mormonism (known as the Church of Jesus Christ of Latter-Day Saints) is also regarded by many Christians as a cult because of its reliance on divine revelations purportedly given to a man named Joseph Smith. Many Christians consider these new revelations to be "another gospel."

Obviously this is merely a sampling of cults; many more exist, and new ones, it seems, spring up every day. A mind-boggling variety of cults currently operate in the United States and around the world. All are teaching their followers to believe extra-biblical doctrines and to worship false gods, which means they are operating undoubtedly under the auspices of Satan. Some look to their leader as their savior. Some, such as Jehovah's Witnesses, teach a salvation by works: "If you distribute so many pieces of literature, you might get into heaven." Or, "If you chant these words, you might find God."

Other cults add to what the Bible says. They speak of "another revelation" of Jesus. Beware. The apostle Paul rebuked the Christians in Galatia for accepting such foolishness. He wrote, "I am amazed that you are so quickly deserting Him who called you by the grace of Christ, for a different gospel; which is really not another; only there are some who are disturbing you and want to distort the gospel of Christ. But even if we, or an angel from heaven, should preach to you a gospel contrary to what we have preached to you, he is to be accursed!" (Gal. 1:6–8). Paul did not take the matter of false teaching lightly, and neither should you.

The main thing to remember about cult members is that they have been deceived. It will do little good to argue with them. The best thing you can do is show them the scriptures that tell who Jesus is and that He died for our sins (John 3:16;, Acts 4:12; and others). Keep pointing the person to the Bible as the absolute authority, not your church or a pastor or television preacher.

Remember: "There is salvation in no one else; for there is no other name under heaven that has been given among men by which we must be saved" (Acts 4:12).

WHAT IS THE OCCULT?

Many people use the terms *cult* and *occult* synonymously. While both types of groups share an aversion to the Lord Jesus Christ, and both are satanically inspired and overlap in some instances, they are not really the same.

The term *occult* is a catchall term used to cover a variety of anti-Christian, demonic activities. The word means "secret" or "concealed."[4] Some occult activities seem harmless at first, but they open the door to deeper involvement. Since these practices are demonic or encouraged by the devil, as a Christian you will want to avoid the following:

Reading horoscopes. This is part of a practice known as *astrology*. Astrology is often mistaken for astronomy, which is a scientific study of the stars. Astrology is not a science. It is the belief that your future can be told by studying the position of the sun, moon, stars, and planets.

Horoscopes offer advice based on a chart with the signs of

the zodiac, an imaginary path that the planets supposedly travel. Much of this advice is general and could apply to almost anyone. For example: "Today you will have an important decision to make. Make it wisely." You probably have important decisions to make every day!

On the other hand, any time you look for future direction apart from God, demonic spirits may be influencing the ones providing those answers. The Bible warns against astrology and future-revealing means: "If there is found among you...a man or a woman...who has gone and served other gods and worshiped them, either the sun or moon or any of the host of heaven...then you shall bring out to your gates that man or woman who has committed that wicked thing, and shall stone to death that man or woman with stones (Deut. 17:2–5, NKJV). Today we don't punish people by stoning them, but you get the picture that God is not pleased with astrology or those who practice it.

God said something similar through His prophet Isaiah. His words have a sarcastic tone to them: "Let now the astrologers, the stargazers, and the monthly prognosticators stand up and save you from what shall come upon you. Behold, they shall be as stubble, the fire shall burn them; they shall not deliver themselves from the power of the flame.... No one shall save you" (Isa. 47:13–15, NKJV).

Also avoid:

Fortune-telling. Fortune tellers claim to be able to tell you about your future by reading your palms, looking into a glass ball, or reading tea leaves or tarot cards. Granted, many of these may be charlatans, but the real thing does exist.

Clairvoyance, mental telepathy, ESP, and psychic powers. This is the belief that certain people have "extrasensory" abilities. They may be able to read somebody's mind or "sense" when something is going to happen. Watch out for anything or anyone that promises to increase, develop, or tap your psychic powers.

Witchcraft and spiritism. Witchcraft is an old, false, anti-Christian system of rituals and chants. Witches claim they can contact and use powers from the unseen world. Spiritists are similar in that they make contact with the dead through a "medium." Those who practice witchcraft are included in Paul's list of people who will not be a part of God's forever family (Gal. 5:19–21).

Satanism. Any worship of the devil or asking him for help is very dangerous. Satan is the enemy of God. Nobody who takes spiritual warfare seriously should ever fraternize with the enemy.

Occult-inspired games. Ouija boards, *Dungeons & Dragons*, and other fantasy role-playing games can also be doorways to trouble. The same can be said for many demon-centered video games.

DIAL-A-DEMON

A relatively recent development in the occult world is the mass marketing of psychic experience. No longer are psychics relegated to sleazy-looking roadside shacks with a "Palm Reader" sign out front. On the contrary, psychics, fortune-tellers, tarot card readers, and other occult practitioners are touted on television and are as close as your telephone or computer. Many of these programs use familiar stars from the movie, television, and music fields to endorse their spiritual "help."

Often these programs and websites have innocuous names such as the National Care Line, which has used as its lead advertising line Jesus's words, "The truth shall make you free." Yes, it will, but the "truth" these people are pitching is neither true nor free. Other programs are more direct in their approach, with names such as Live Psychic Chat, Psychic Friends Networks (these psychics are not your friends), Psychic Support Group, or The Psychic Foundation.

At least you don't have to guess where they are coming from. Their television infomercials glowingly report success stories such as lost babies who were found through the assistance of psychics, crimes that were solved, or lovelorn single men and women, disgruntled with dating, who were brought together with the mate of their dreams through psychic networking. It all sounds too good to be true...and it is.

You need to understand that these programs are not simply parlor games; many of them are downright demonic, whether the people involved with them realize it or not. If you pick up the phone to call that program or go to that website online, you may as well dial 1-900-LUCIFER. You will be dialing up a hotline to hell. Don't even watch the programs or visit the websites. Not that you have anything to fear from the content (other than your intelligence being insulted), but why ask someone to pour dirt all over your spirit?

With computer technology expanding exponentially every year, the devil is now high-tech, using computer modems to tap into many unsuspecting victims' hearts and minds. As with most great technology, the Internet can be used for good or evil. The latter has not escaped Satan's notice. Consequently you can go directly online with a demon or hook into a vast array of occult services as close as your monitor. Clearly this is not the kind of progress deemed helpful to your spiritual life.

Understand: the Bible never says that these occult activities are silly little party games. Nor does it say that they do not work. The Bible simply says to stay away from them. God wants you to get the direction for your life from Him, and He pulls no punches concerning those who seek out other sources of spiritual insight:

There shall not be found among you anyone who makes his son or his daughter pass through the fire, one who uses divination, one who practices witchcraft, or one who interprets omens, or a sorcerer, or one who casts a spell, or a medium, or a spiritist, or one who calls up the dead. For whoever does these things is detestable to the LORD; and because of these detestable things the LORD your God will drive them out before you. You shall be blameless before the LORD your God. For those nations, which you shall dispossess, listen to those who practice witchcraft and to diviners, but as for you, the LORD your God has not allowed you to do so.

—DEUTERONOMY 18:10–14

Mediums, spiritists, people who interpret omens, and all other types of divination—whether they look into a crystal ball or tap into your computer—will all have their place in eternity…and it won't be heaven. With "friends" like these…

BEWARE OF SATANIC TRINKETS

By now you have probably realized that this is not a "seeing demons everywhere" type of book. With that disclaimer in mind, let me caution you concerning the keeping of any item of clothing, jewelry, literature, art objects, charms, or other materials that may have at one time been connected with demonic activity. If you even think an item has a demonic history, get rid of it. Although the item itself has no power (remember Paul's words about the idols in 1 Corinthians 10:19), frequently the people who have made the materials or used them have dedicated them to the devil, and an evil spirit seems to remain with the item. Perhaps that is why the people in Ephesus who came to Jesus out of a past filled with black magic instinctively decided to burn the items they had previously used in demonic worship (Acts 19:19).

As a student at a secular university I was assigned to do a term paper on the occult. I was a relatively new Christian with a lot of zeal and little wisdom, so I enthusiastically plunged in "where angels fear to tread." I loaded my desk with occult literature that I used to research my subject. One book written by a leader in the Church of Satan (yes, there really is such a thing) was especially informative.

As I plodded my way through the term paper, I found myself becoming more and more lethargic about life. I was tired and irritable most of the time and indifferent toward others around me. When the paper was finally finished and turned in, I discarded all of my notes and returned my resource materials to the library or to my friends from whom I had borrowed them. All except that one book. I didn't read it or refer to it in any way. I merely left it on my bookshelf.

I continued in a state of deep depression for several weeks following that project. I wasn't physically sick. I had experienced no major calamities in my life that had burdened me. I even got an A on the paper. Still, I couldn't shake the darkness enveloping my life. Then one day I was looking on my bookshelf and discovered the book that I had purchased was written by a Satanist. As a new Christian I didn't have a clue about spiritual warfare, but I sensed the Holy Spirit speaking to my heart and mind, saying, "Get rid of that book."

I grabbed the book and took it downstairs in my parents' home and threw it into the furnace. I stood watching with the furnace door open as the flames licked around the book and slowly consumed it. As that book went up in smoke, so did my depression. I sensed it lifting off me almost immediately, and I have never experienced anything similar since that time.

Was the lifting of that depression a coincidence? I don't think so. I have now come to believe that when I bought that book, a spirit came with it. The spirit most likely would have hung around my life as long as the book was in my possession.

In all our lives we possess a lot of excess baggage, some of which we pull into our Christian experience from our pre-Christian lifestyles. If any item seems to possess unusual influence or power in your life, get rid of it. It's not worth it. As a Christian you don't need good-luck charms, "fairy dust," or any other object for your protection or provision. You have the Lord God Jehovah-Jireh, the Hebrew name which means "the Lord will provide."

WHAT'S THE NEW AGE RAGE?

Many Christians and non-Christians alike are confused about the New Age movement. The New Age movement is not a gang of anti-Christian raiders out to destroy your faith. It is not even a well-organized group. Sadly it is simply another of Satan's twisted attempts to deceive those who are seeking spiritual truth.

Still, the New Age movement is dangerous. While it has no distinct doctrine, the New Age falls into the cult category because it denies Jesus Christ is God. Most forms of New Age teaching say, sooner or later, that *we* are gods. Beyond that the movement believes that *everything* is god. Ironically the New Age is not really new at all. It is a weird amalgamation of ancient teachings based on Hinduism, Buddhism, other Eastern religions, and the occult. In a way it is little more than old-fashioned pantheism.

From ancient history people have worshipped rocks, trees, animals, clouds, volcanoes, people, and all sorts of objects. It is all idol worship, worshipping the created order rather than the Creator. But think about it: if Satan simply had named the New Age movement "The Same Old Stupid Lies That We've Been

Falling for These Past Two Thousand Years," nobody would have wanted anything to do with it.

Satan wanted to be equal with God, and he was thrown out of heaven as a result. The devil duped Adam and Eve into making the same mistake of wanting to be like God. Ever since, people have tried to be their own gods. But we are not God. We are created beings. Only God is God.

Satan lures people into believing that by meditating and making use of their own inner potential, they can have godlike powers. Thousands have been deceived into thinking that they can "save" themselves. Others believe that a "Christ" will come, bringing peace and prosperity to the world. But they are not talking about Jesus.

The danger of the New Age is that some of it sounds similar to biblical teaching. In every lie there is a kernel of truth. If a person doesn't know the truth of God's Word, he or she can easily be misled. In the days ahead don't be surprised if more books, movies, and music have "spiritual" themes. But the "spirit" will not be the Holy Spirit. It will be a spirit spawned in hell.

SOME COMMON NEW AGE PRACTICES

New Agers practice a variety of strange rites, such as yoga, meditation, spiritual chanting, out-of-body experiences, and many more activities, so it is difficult to give an exhaustive list. Here are a few of the more familiar practices often associated with New Age "religions":

Channeling. Channelers are people who claim to have or to be "spirit guides." They insist that the spirit of someone who died can pass information (channeling information) through them back to you. The Bible says to stay away from this stuff. The Word is clear: "There shall not be found among you anyone who...practices witchcraft, or a soothsayer, or one who interprets omens, or a sorcerer, or one who conjures spells, or a medium, or a spiritist, or one who calls up the dead" (Deut. 18:10–11, NKJV).

Channelers often speak about "opening up to a higher self." Watch out. The only higher self you want to open to is Jesus.

Crystals. Many believers in the New Age have a collection of crystals that they place in their homes, their purses, and their cars. These people are not merely collectors of fancy rocks. They believe the crystals have power. They say some crystals can heal diseases; others, they believe, will bring you health, love, peace, or money. Strange, isn't it? People who used to laugh at "mood rings" are now buying colored stones to bring them the happiness that only God can give.

Holistic health practices. Again, many of these ideas sound good at first. But if you look carefully, you will find occult practices. Beware of health practices such as biofeedback, hypnosis, some forms of acupuncture, and psychic healing. These practices too are frequently laced with Eastern mysticism. They often involve "mind over matter" activities, as well as the surrender of your will to another human being.

Many New Age devotees also believe in reincarnation, a Hindu idea of being reborn as different people or animals until you finally get your life right. Don't worry, they say, if you blow it in this life. There is no hell; there is no heaven, just another go-around here on earth. If you mess up in the next life, maybe you will do better in the next or the next.

THE WORST DANGER OF ALL

While the dangers of these false religions are obvious even with such a cursory review, the New Age's worst danger is that it keeps people who are sincerely seeking spiritual truth from finding the real thing—a relationship with Jesus. They have gotten sidetracked into a New Age pit, and many are stuck in a spiritual quicksand that is sucking them down to destruction.

Nobody has ever found God through the New Age. They may have found a god made in man's image or some other image. Others may have found the Lord despite New Age teaching. But the New Age religions cannot save anyone. They have no power to do so.

No one will ever have his or her sins forgiven through the New Age movement. Nobody will go to heaven as a result of the New Age religions. No one has been or ever will be reincarnated. The Bible says, "It is appointed for men to die once and after this comes judgment" (Heb. 9:27).

But the New Age is not going to go away. It is here to stay. More than ever before, modern Christians need to know what they believe and why. With so many people seeking spiritual truth, God may be able to use you to point New Agers to Jesus Christ, the One who said, "I am the Truth."

GET UNHOOKED

If you are currently involved with any of Satan's "hooks," or if sexual sins, alcohol or drug abuse, occult practices, or involvement in a cult or New Age group have been part of your past, you may need deliverance from demonic activity. This does not lessen your own responsibility for your actions, but it might help explain why you have been experiencing such difficulty in overcoming certain sins.

First, ask God to show you if demonic activity is involved in the situation with which you are dealing. Don't go making up demons where they don't exist, and never try to blame a demon for sinful actions for which you are solely responsible. Ask the Holy Spirit to make it clear to you who or what is responsible and what, if anything, you should do.

Second, seek help from your pastor or a professional counselor who acknowledges the possibility of demonic oppression and is willing to pray with you for your deliverance. You can take authority in the name of Jesus over the devil and his demons, and you don't need a prayer partner for that. But if deliverance from demonic oppression is necessary, I strongly encourage you to seek help.

In most cases, though, you will not need outside help. You simply must submit to God and resist the devil. Most spiritual warfare battles are won on our knees. I call it victory in surrender. Let me show you what I mean.

Chapter Eighteen

VICTORY IN SURRENDER

T IFFANY, A HIGH school physics teacher, and her colleagues were in trouble. They were trying to take authority over an evil spirit they felt had infiltrated their school, causing many members of the faculty and administration to have an antichrist spirit. But no matter what Tiffany and her friends did, they were met with failure. Their voluntary, student-led Bible club—for which they served as sponsors—had been meeting for several years in the school auditorium during activities period, but all of a sudden school officials disallowed it as a violation of laws ostensibly separating church and state.

When the school board passed a decree that banned the teaching of "creation science" as an alternative to the theory of evolution, Tiffany and her colleagues tried again to resist the devil in Jesus's name. Along with more than a hundred students they gathered around the school flagpole before the start of school one morning and rebuked the devil. But nothing happened.

Spiritually frustrated and feeling like foolish failures, Tiffany and her friends retreated. As they backed away from their public testimonies, however, the devil launched a counterattack. Tiffany and her fellow Christian teachers were ostracized by their colleagues, mocked by many people in the community, and called before the administrative board to give account of their actions to ensure they were not attempting to convert students to Christianity. "The school is no place to be expressing your religious viewpoints," they were told repeatedly.

Disappointed and dejected, Tiffany groused, "What went wrong? We resisted the devil in Jesus's name, and we were devastated as a result."

WHAT WENT WRONG?

What indeed? Tiffany's experience is not unique. Frequently well-meaning Christians encounter a situation in which they are certain demonic activity is taking place. In a rush of enthusiasm (often after hearing teaching about spiritual warfare or reading a book such as this on the subject) they leap headlong into an attack upon satanic strongholds. With little planning, preparation, and, most dangerous of all, little prayer, they assume that Satan is going to roll over and play dead because of their efforts. When it doesn't happen that way, the zealous spiritual warriors limp away wondering what hit them, often with their faith shattered. Why does this happen?

The number one reason for defeat in spiritual battles with the enemy and his demons is a misunderstanding of our priorities. James 4:7 explicitly states, "Submit therefore to God. Resist the devil and he will flee from you."

Notice the order: submit to God first then resist the devil. Most of us reverse that order. Whenever the devil begins launching his flaming missiles, the first thing we do is normally a knee-jerk response to the enemy. Right there what we ought to do is surrender the situation to God. First, acknowledge afresh that Jesus Christ is Lord in your life. Declare aloud that He is Lord of the situation you are facing. Seek the Lord's direction and timing as to how you should resist the devil.

Satan loves it whenever we attempt to come against him in a spirit of independence and pride rather than in a spirit of dependence upon the Lord Jesus and humility before each other. But when Christians humble themselves before God and one another, repenting of our sins, the devil knows he doesn't stand a chance.

During the 1978 World Cup Soccer Games held in Cordoba, Argentina, John Dawson led a group of two hundred Youth With A Mission (YWAM) members in an evangelistic outreach on the streets of Cordoba. The team preached in the streets and passed out gospel literature. Most people attending the games, however, paid little attention to their preaching and even less to the literature, most of which got tossed aside with hardly a glance.

John and the YWAM team were frustrated and discouraged, so several of the leaders met to pray. As they did, God showed them that they were battling a spirit of pride that permeated Cordoba and was manifested in the city's reputation for sophistication, possessions, and upscale appearances. The Spirit of God also began to deal with the YWAM leaders' own pride and their concern for appearances.

Dawson and the other leaders humbled themselves before God and repented, confessing specific areas of their own pride and asking the Lord to cleanse their hearts. Then they went to their two hundred coworkers and humbled themselves before them. As the YWAM team submitted to the Lord and repented of their own pride, the Lord gave them a new strategy to be used in resisting the devil.

The YWAM team scattered throughout the city—on the streets, at the stadium, and in the central shopping mall. They knelt down right in front of some of Cordoba's most elegant shops and began to pray, repenting of their own sins and those of the city. Immediately the team members saw a change. Instead of tossing aside their gospel tracts, people now asked the missionaries for more, even asking them to autograph them.

Instead of ignoring the gospel preaching, people in the crowd at the Plaza of San Martin dropped to their knees, repenting of their sins as John Dawson and the other team members preached the good news. For the next several weeks people continued to seek out the YWAM members, asking how they could be saved from their sins. Satan's hold on Cordoba had been broken, not through the power of persuasion or the loud shouting down of the enemy but through humility, repentance, and prayer.[1]

Perhaps that is what it will take to break the bondage in your life or in your church or city—or in our nation. Nevertheless, here again, don't look at these weapons of spiritual warfare as magic formulas. The "secret" is to submit to God. Do whatever He tells you, and then resist the devil. The Lord will bring about the success as He sees fit.

THREE STEPS TO VICTORY

If a formula for spiritual success exists in the Bible, it is John's triumphant words in the Book of Revelation concerning those Christians who overcame the "accuser of our brethren." Interestingly John is writing prophetically about the future, but he reports this vision in the past tense. In other words, he could well be talking about you and me. John writes: "And they overcame him because of the blood of the Lamb and because of the word of their testimony, and they did not love their life even when faced with death" (Rev. 12:11).

THE BLOOD OF JESUS

Satan hates to be reminded about the blood of Jesus. It was by "the blood of the Lamb" shed on Calvary that Jesus disarmed Satan's principalities and powers, rulers and authorities, and made a public spectacle of them (Col. 2:15). The blood of Jesus remains an embarrassment to the devil to this day. Demons will shy away from anybody or anything that is "covered by the blood of Jesus."

Consider this: I hate bugs, so every month I have a pesticide company spray our home to prevent the bugs from coming into the house. The spray my bug man uses creates an invisible barrier around all the entrances, windows, and cracks in our home. When a bug approaches, you can actually see him (or her?) sense the invisible protection and turn away. If a bug is stupid enough to cross that invisible line, he's dead. The residual effects of the spray will kill him.

Forgive me for such a crude illustration, but something similar happens when demons approach anyone or anything covered by the blood of Jesus. The devil or his demons may approach, but when they sense the blood, they back away in fear for their lives.

The members of my family pray daily, "Lord Jesus, cover me [us] with Your blood." We pray that way whether we are at home, riding in a car across town, or getting onto an airplane halfway around the world. We pray similarly before going to bed every night. We aren't using the blood of Jesus as a magic formula; we are basically asking the Lord to reapply His blood to our lives and circumstances.

Frankly I don't feel that Jesus requires us to do that. As far as He is concerned, He purchased us with His blood and applied the blood to our hearts. We belong to Him. But we need that reminder. We need the fresh application of the blood of the Lamb to cover our failures, foibles, and sins. Furthermore we have found that it certainly does not hurt to "check all the flaps" before entering a fight with the enemy. We need the blood of the Lamb as our invisible protective covering.

The blood of Jesus is one of the most potent weapons you have in spiritual warfare. Do you remember the old song "There's Power in the Blood"? Well, it's true. There really is power in the blood: power to save us, power to heal us, power to protect us from demonic oppression.

How do you "use" the blood of Jesus as a weapon? The next time Satan gives you any trouble, just remind him of what the blood of Jesus means. For example, when Satan says, "You are nothing but a filthy sinner. You cannot pray; you should not expect God to give you the time of day," just turn around and say something like, "The Word of God tells me that my sins are forgiven, and now anytime I want, I can have 'confidence to enter the holy place by the blood of Jesus'" (Heb. 10:19). Another important scripture you might use against the devil is: "The blood of Jesus His Son cleanses us from all sin" (1 John 1:7).

Start quoting scriptures about the blood of Jesus to Satan. The devil hates that. If you can't remember any verses, read some aloud. Of course, this is a good reason you should make it a habit to memorize key passages of Scripture. I also mark in the front of my Bible important verses I might need in combating the devil in specific situations.

Why should we speak or quote scriptures about the blood of Jesus to the devil? By holding the blood of Christ over the devil's head, it makes current the victory of the cross. It reminds the devil that he is nothing more than a created being, that Jesus Christ defeated him on the cross, and that the blood of Jesus is still sufficient to overcome him. Satan has no recourse but to slink away in shame when he is confronted by the blood of Jesus—especially when it is combined with the Word of God.

The Word of Their Testimony

When you declare the truth about Jesus Christ and what He has done for you and can do for others, the devil cringes. It is like rubbing salt in his wounds. This is offensive spiritual warfare, not simply defending against demonic attacks but standing up and fighting back, taking territory for God.

Frequently you must refute the negative reports of the enemy by testifying in faith. A fascinating account of spiritual warfare is recorded in three separate places in Scripture (2 Kings 18–19; 2 Chron. 32:1–23; Isa. 36–37). God's people, led by King

Hezekiah, were being held under siege by King Sennacherib of Assyria. The enemy had already seized the major fortified cities of Judah, and the Assyrians were now putting heavy pressure on Jerusalem, the capital city. In true satanic form Sennacherib demanded a hefty ransom from God's people and then sent his emissary, Rabshakeh, to intimidate Hezekiah into making a deal. Each day Rabshakeh stood outside the city walls, yelling insults toward Hezekiah, toward God, and toward His people.

When several of Hezekiah's emissaries went out to meet with the enemy king's representative, Rabshakeh railed against them, saying, "What is this confidence that you have? You say that you have counsel and strength for war, but those are only empty words. Where do you guys come off rebelling against me?" Rabshakeh's ultimate attempted deception came when he said, "Have I now come up without the Lord's approval against this place to destroy it? The LORD said to me, 'Go up against this land and destroy it'" (2 Kings 18:25).

Can you believe this guy? He is the emissary of Satan's king, telling God's people that the Lord sent him there to destroy them. He's saying, "God told me to do this."

Hezekiah's emissaries attempted to prevent God's oppressed people from hearing Rabshakeh's insults by requesting that he speak in Aramaic rather than Hebrew, but Rabshakeh refused. He raised his voice and began ranting all the more, presenting three "logical reasons" God's people should submit to Sennacherib.

First, he roared, "Hear the word of the great king, the king of Assyria.... 'Do not let Hezekiah deceive you, for he will not be able to deliver you from my hand; nor let Hezekiah make you trust in the LORD, saying, 'The LORD will surely deliver us, and this city will not be given into the hand of the king of Assyria'" (2 Kings 18:28–30).

Second, Rabshakeh tempted God's people by telling them,

"Come make a bargain, make your peace with me. We'll take good care of you. We'll give you food to eat, a land of bread and vineyards. Each of you can have your own place where you can live it up." (See 2 Kings 18:31–32.) No doubt, to the tired, hungry, besieged people of God listening on the wall to Rabshakeh's words, the enemy's deal sounded mighty enticing. Finally Rabshakeh rationalized the matter saying, "Look, have any of the gods of other nations delivered anyone from the hand of the king of Assyria? No, none of them. What makes you think you are any different?" (See 2 Kings 18:33–35.)

Understand, the devil will tell you absolutely anything if he thinks it will help lead you to destruction. Sometimes he will even tell the truth if it advances his hellish purposes.

Hezekiah had warned God's people not to do verbal battle with the enemy, and the people obeyed Hezekiah's command. When the king got word of Rabshakeh's taunts, he tore his clothes and covered himself with sackcloth as signs of both his heartrending grief and his humility before God. Then Hezekiah went into the house of the Lord to pray.

No doubt, had Hezekiah thrown up his hands in despair, the battle would have been all over for God's people. But Hezekiah didn't do that. Instead he submitted to God, and he testified of God's greatness. Notice too that he resisted the enemy by first refusing to respond in foolish verbal confrontations, and then he diffused the enemy's threats by taking them to the Lord in prayer.

When he prayed, Hezekiah did not begin outlining his woeful dilemma to God. He began by praising God. He said, "O LORD, the God of Israel, who are enthroned above the cherubim, You are the God, You alone, of all the kingdoms of the earth. You have made heaven and earth" (2 Kings 19:15).

With the devil beating on his door, Hezekiah paused to praise the Lord and testified of His awesome power before asking Him for help. Then he sent for the prophet Isaiah, hoping that Isaiah would have a word from the Lord.

Isaiah did. He told Hezekiah's emissaries to tell the king, "Thus says the LORD, 'Do not be afraid because of the words that you have heard, with which the servants of the king of Assyria have blasphemed Me. Behold, I will put a spirit in him so that he will hear a rumor and return to his own land. And I will make him fall by the sword in his own land'" (Isa. 37:6–7).

Shortly after this Sennacherib mysteriously received word that Babylon was in rebellion. He suddenly abandoned his siege of Jerusalem and headed his army homeward, toward modern-day Baghdad. But God wasn't finished with Sennacherib yet. Nobody blasphemes Almighty God and gets away with it for long. "Then the angel of the LORD went out and struck 185,000 in the camp of the Assyrians; and when men arose early in the morning, behold, all of these were dead" (v. 36).

Sennacherib, the devil's man, returned home defeated and eventually was murdered by his own sons. Hezekiah and the people of God won a great victory by surrendering the battle to the Lord.

If you ever have any doubts about how strong the angel of the Lord is, let this account cause faith to well up in your heart. One angel destroyed 185,000 of the devil's finest warriors overnight. And the Bible says, "The angel of the LORD encamps around those who fear Him" (Ps. 34:7). Repeatedly the Scripture says there are angels all around us. Furthermore the prophet Elisha said, "Do not fear, for those who are with us are more than those who are with them" (2 Kings 6:16). These angels are "ministering spirits, sent out to render service for the sake of those who will inherit salvation" (Heb. 1:14). Besides that, the Bible indicates that God has assigned guardian angels to protect and help each of us (Matt. 18:10).

Knowing that you have the devil's demons outnumbered can

give you a sense of boldness in spiritual warfare, and it should. But nowhere in the Bible are we instructed to put our faith in angels. Our confidence is in Jesus Christ.

Praise as a spiritual weapon

The Bible is replete with commands for God's people to testify of God's excellent greatness and to praise Him. Those who do, discover that praise is a powerful weapon in spiritual warfare. Praise is not merely mouthing the words "Praise the Lord." Nor is it simply singing choruses and songs about Jesus. It is entering into a heartfelt attitude of worship and exaltation of the Lord. You may sing, shout, dance, raise your hands, or manifest a variety of other external expressions, but praise, if it is to be genuine, must begin in your heart, in your spirit.

There really is power in this sort of praise, probably even more than we realize. For example, Psalm 149 reveals praise as a spiritual weapon:

> Let the godly ones exalt in glory;
> Let them sing for joy on their beds.
> Let the high praises of God be in their mouth.
> And a two-edged sword in their hand,
> To execute vengeance on the nations
> And punishment on the peoples,
> To bind their kings with chains
> And their nobles with fetters of iron,
> To execute on them the judgment written;
> This is an honor for all His godly ones.
> Praise the Lord!
>
> —PSALM 149:5–9

This passage describes a spiritual battle; it is not a rationale for Christians to bomb abortion clinics, assassinate political figures, or attempt to overthrow governments. In fact, rather than physical confrontation with the enemies of God, throughout the

Bible we are instructed to pray for them, praise the Lord, and leave the rest up to God. Granted, at times in the Scriptures we read of God's people having to physically fight. Frequently, however, we find that real victories can be won without lifting a finger.

The account of Jehoshaphat, king of Judah, is a wonderful illustration of this. King Jehoshaphat was facing an impending attack by an overwhelming enemy army. The king was unashamedly afraid, but he did the right thing; he "turned his attention to seek the LORD" (2 Chron. 20:3). As he did, he stood up and publicly exalted the Lord before the people of the land. He said, "O LORD, the God of our fathers, are You not God in the heavens? And are You not ruler over all the kingdoms of the nations? Power and might are in Your hand so that no one can stand against You" (v. 6).

As the people of God prayed along with Jehoshaphat, the Spirit of the Lord came upon a man named Jahaziel, and he prophesied: "Listen, all Judah and the inhabitants of Jerusalem and King Jehoshaphat: thus says the LORD to you, 'Do not fear or be dismayed because of this great multitude, for the battle is not yours but God's'" (v. 15).

The Lord gave Jehoshaphat and the people specific instructions concerning the upcoming battle. The next day God's people went out to battle the enemy, not with swords and spears but with praise and worship to the Lord. Jehoshaphat appointed "those who sang to the LORD and those who praised Him in holy attire" to lead the army, singing and praising God, saying, "Give thanks to the LORD, for His lovingkindness is everlasting" (v. 21).

As the people began singing and praising, the Lord set ambushes for the enemies, and they were routed (v. 22). Author Dean Sherman comments upon this passage: "As Jehoshaphat's praise warriors raised their voices to God, angels were sent to defeat a physical foe. The physical enemy was defeated because unseen enemies were scattered by the power of praise."[2]

As you proclaim the word of your testimony, giving praise to God for who He is and what He has done for you, any demonic enemies trying to attack you will be driven back. The way to drive back the darkness of the devil is by letting your light shine for Jesus!

DON'T BE AFRAID TO DIE

The third key to success in spiritual warfare is "they did not love their life even when faced with death" (Rev. 12:11). In other words, the victorious heroes John is describing were not afraid to lay their lives on the line for the Lord Jesus.

We have not seen many heroes of that caliber in our ranks lately. Corrie ten Boom was one. You owe it to yourself to read her book or watch the movie *The Hiding Place*. Corrie grew up in the Netherlands, and the world might never have heard of her had not a demonic maniac arisen in Germany. Early in his regime Adolf Hitler determined to exterminate the Jewish people from his Third Reich. When his secret police, the Gestapo, began rounding up the Jewish people in the Netherlands and shipping them off to death camps, Corrie ten Boom and her family decided they had to do something.

Despite the possible punishment, and at great personal risk to themselves, Corrie's family sheltered as many Jewish people from the Nazis as possible, helping many to escape to freedom. Eventually Corrie and her family were arrested. Their father died in prison ten days after his arrest. Corrie and her sister Betsie were ultimately condemned to the horror chambers of Ravensbrück concentration camp. There they suffered unspeakable personal humiliation, pain, and torture, and Betsie died; Corrie herself barely made it out alive, a walking skeleton.[3]

And for what? Why did they do what they did? Because they loved Jesus more than they loved their own lives.

Nowadays one of Satan's most effective weapons against lukewarm, situation-ethics-saturated Christians is the life-threatening circumstance. "You better not try to come against me," he warns, "or I will kill you." Most Christians who are not accustomed to spiritual warfare or the devil's loud-mouthed bluffing tactics back off immediately.

"Keep your mouth shut about Jesus," Satan warns, "or you will lose your job or get tossed out of school."

"Stay out of the arts, entertainment, and sports fields; those are mine," the devil lies. "Stay out of the media and out of politics. Those belong to me too. Keep your faith at church where it belongs, or in your homes. Leave the other areas to me."

Sadly many Christians have cowered and run away in fear at the first sign of Satan's threats. But God is raising a shrewd army of Christians in these days, men and women who recognize the devil for who and what he is—a deceiver, a liar, a defeated foe, and a bluffer. This group of believers is armed with the Word of God, confident in Christ, and filled with the Holy Spirit.

When Satan says, "I'll kill you if you try to take the gospel there," these bold believers turn right around and say, "Go ahead, devil. You can't hurt me. All you can do is hasten my ride home."

But that doesn't mean you will never again have to face fear. It simply means your love for Jesus will overcome it. At the height of Idi Amin's mad attempt to rid Uganda of Christians in late 1972, the demonic dictator killed more than ninety thousand innocent people in less than three months. Kefa Sempangi pastored a large Christian church in Uganda, so he and the Christians who worshipped together there were prime targets for Amin's madness.

Amin's soldiers struck with inhuman savagery on a whim. One family, living in a wealthy section of Kampala, was attacked in the middle of the day while the entire family was home. Amin's soldiers burst into the house, rounded up the family, and then seized the father. After forcing him to submit to unspeakable atrocities, they slashed off his hands and raped his wife while he lay dying. The soldiers plundered the house, taking whatever they wanted, and then climbed into their army van and left, laughing uproariously. Friends and family members brought the traumatized widow to the pastor. Her face was swollen, and she was covered with bruises; she was emotionally paralyzed, and her eyes were locked in a blank stare.

Sempangi and some of the elders of the church prayed for the woman, and she was miraculously healed. Two weeks later she and her children and their relatives sat in the front row at church. It was a remarkable recovery, and God used the miracle to bring many more people to Jesus.

Still, with the awful memories of the woman's bruised face and her husband's dismembered body fresh in his mind, Pastor Sempangi was understandably struck by stark terror when, on Easter Sunday, five of Amin's soldiers strode into his church office, brandishing their rifles in his face and announcing they were going to kill him.

A tall man spoke quietly but hatefully to Sempangi, "If you have something to say, say it before you die." Later Sempangi recounted his feelings at that moment:

> I could only stare at him. For a sickening moment I felt the full weight of his rage. We had never met before but his deepest desire was to tear me to pieces. My mouth felt heavy and my limbs began to shake.... *They will not need to kill me*, I thought to myself...*I am just going to fall over dead and I will never see my family again.*...From far away I heard a voice, and I was astonished to realize that it was my own. "I do not need to plead my own cause," I heard myself saying. "I am a

dead man already. My life is dead and hidden in Christ. It is your lives that are in danger; you are dead in your sins. I will pray to God that after you have killed me, He will spare you from eternal destruction." The tall one took a step toward me and then stopped. In an instant his face was changed. His hatred turned to curiosity.... Then the tall one spoke again. "Will you pray for us now?" he asked.[4]

Sempangi prayed a simple prayer for the soldiers, asking God to forgive them for their sins. As the pastor prayed, he fully expected to be shot to death at any moment. But when he finished and looked up at the men, he recognized that something had changed in their faces. The tall man motioned to the others, and the five soldiers walked out, leaving Sempangi and his family unharmed.

A few weeks later the tall soldier walked into Sempangi's office once again. Instinctively the pastor felt the same fear for his life as he had known when looking down the barrel of the soldier's gun during their first meeting. Again, the soldier surprised him. "Now that I am a born-again one," he asked, "what do I do next?"

The pastor learned later that the soldier had murdered over two hundred people with his own hands. He told Sempangi, "All this time, I thought I was working for Amin, but I have been working for Satan." Then the soldier told the pastor the rest of his story:

"When we came to kill you Easter morning," he said, "we were going to kill you in front of everyone. We were going to show you our power. But we kept sitting in the service. I didn't hear anything you said; I could only see the widows and orphans around me. Some of them I knew. I had killed their men with my own hands, and I expected them to be weeping and mourning. But they were clapping, they were singing songs, and they were happy. Their joy made me so afraid. I thought to myself, if for one moment I could understand it, I would give up everything. When we came to this room and you prayed for us, I did understand. I felt something in my life I had never felt before."[5]

Pastor Sempangi prayed for the soldier that he might find full forgiveness for his sins, even though they were awful and many. The man did. Not only did he find the love of Jesus, but he also brought his four buddies, and they found Christ as well.

That is spiritual warfare, and that kind of confidence, even in the face of death, is what the apostle John was talking about when he wrote, "And they overcame him because of the blood of the Lamb and because of the word of their testimony, and they did not love their life even when faced with death" (Rev. 12:11).

In the days ahead, each of us will be called upon to take our stand for Jesus Christ and to boldly resist the devil. That is the battle to which we are called, each in our own way. Be bold! Be courageous. The battle is the Lord's, and in the name of Jesus we are more than conquerors. We can stand up and fight back.

May God protect you and bless you as you do!

NOTES

Chapter Two
Snake in the Grass

1. C. Peter Wagner, *Engaging the Enemy* (Ventura, CA: Regal, 1991), xiii.

2. Dean Sherman, *Spiritual Warfare for Every Christian* (Seattle, WA: YWAM Publishing, 1992), 28.

Chapter Three
Where Did Satan Come From?

1. Dennis J. Hester, *The Vance Havner Notebook* (Grand Rapids, MI: Baker Book House, 1989).

2. LaMar Boschman, *The Rebirth of Music* (Shippensburg, PA: Destiny Image Publishers, 2000), 4.

3. Thinkexist.com, "Flip Wilson quotes," http://thinkexist.com/quotes/flip_wilson/ (accessed October 15, 2012).

4. Wikipedia.com, "The Church Lady," http://en.wikipedia.org/wiki/The_Church_Lady (accessed October 16, 2012).

5. Emory Stevens Buck, gen. ed., *Interpreter's Dictionary of the Bible* (Nashville, TN: Abingdon, 1962), 52.

Chapter Four
How Did We Get Involved?

1. Winkie Pratney, *The Thomas Factor* (Old Tapan, NJ: Chosen, 1989), 86.

Chapter Six
Passing the Point of No Return

1. Cliff Spieler, Jerry Brydges, Don Glynn, and Bill Nelson, *Niagara Falls Gazette*, July 10, 1960, 1.

2. *The Passion of the Christ*, directed by Mel Gibson (Los Angeles: 20th Century Fox Home Entertainment Home Entertainment, 2004), DVD.

3. Sherman, *Spiritual Warfare for Every Christian*.

CHAPTER SEVEN
THE DEVIL'S GAME PLAN

1. Tom Landry with Gregg Lewis, *Tom Landry, An Autobiography* (Grand Rapids, MI: Zondervan, 1990), 100.

2. Ibid, 145.

3. Ed Murphy, *The Handbook for Spiritual Warfare* (Nashville, TN: Thomas Nelson, 1992), 445.

4. I am indebted to Winkie Pratney for his insights on 1 Samuel 11. He spoke at a Last Days Artist Retreat in July 1986. Last Days Ministries is located in Lindale, TX.

CHAPTER EIGHT
BATTLE STATIONS

1. David Seamands, "Temptation" (Pasadena, CA: Tape Ministers, 1976).

CHAPTER NINE
WASH YOUR MOUTH OUT WITH SOAP!

1. Sherman, *Spiritual Warfare for Every Christian.*

2. James Orr, gen. ed., *International Standard Bible Encyclopedia* (Grand Rapids, MI: Wm. B. Eerdmans Publishing Co., 1939), s.v. "curse," http://www.internationalstandardbible.com/C/curse.html (accessed October 17, 2012).

3. Brainy Quote, "Respect Quotes," http://www.brainyquote.com/quotes/keywords/respect_2.html (accessed October 17, 2012).

CHAPTER TEN
THE WRESTLER AND THE WARRIOR

1. Kenneth Wuest, *Ephesians in the Greek New Testament* (Grand Rapids, MI: Eerdmans, 1983).

2. Mark I. Bubeck, *The Adversary* (Chicago, IL: Moody, 1975).

3. Wagner, *Engaging the Enemy.*

4. David Manske, "Death at Midnight," *Alliance Life,* February 19, 1992, 6.

CHAPTER ELEVEN
YOUR WARDROBE AND YOUR WEAPONS

1. Corrie ten Boom, *Not Good If Detached* (Fort Washington, PA: Christian Literature Crusade, 1970).

CHAPTER TWELVE
GUNS AND ROSES

1. Sherman, *Spiritual Warfare for Every Christian*, 132. Viewed at Google Books.

2. Adapted from Jack Taylor, *Much More!* (Nashville, TN: Broadman, 1972), 56–57.

CHAPTER THIRTEEN
DEMONS ON THE RUN

1. Tony Cummings, "Gary S. Paxton: From 'Monster Mash' to 'He's Alive,' an Incredible Journey," Cross Rhythms, September 2, 2011, http://www.crossrhythms.co.uk/articles/music/Gary_S_Paxton_From_Monster_Mash_to_Hes_Alive_an_incredible_journey/44188/p1/ (accessed November 29, 2012).

CHAPTER FOURTEEN
POWER TO BIND, POWER TO LOOSE, POWER TO SPARE!

1. Wagner, *Engaging the Enemy*, 15. Viewed at Google Books.

2. A. W. Tozer, *I Talk Back to the Devil* (Harrisburg, PA: Christian Publications, 1972).

3. Loren Cunningham, *Making Jesus Lord* (Seattle, WA: YWAM Publishing, 1988), 119.

CHAPTER FIFTEEN
THE DEVIL OR THE DOVE

1. V. Raymond Edman, *They Found the Secret* (Grand Rapids, MI: Zondervan, 1984), 14.

2. Ibid., 12, 14.

3. Merrill C. Tenney, gen. ed., *The Zondervan Pictorial Encyclopedia of the Bible* (Grand Rapids, MI: Zondervan Publishing House, 1975), 598.

CHAPTER SIXTEEN
HOW TO BE FILLED WITH THE HOLY SPIRIT

1. As quoted in *365 Daily Treasures of Wisdom* (Uhrichsville, OH: Barbour Pub Inc, 2007).

CHAPTER SEVENTEEN
HOOKS FROM HELL

1. *Hook*, directed by Steven Spielberg (Culver City, CA: Sony Pictures Home Entertainment, 2000), DVD.

2. John C. Danforth, *Final Report to the Deputy Attorney General Concerning the 1993 Confrontation at the Mt. Carmel Complex Waco, Texas*, November 8, 2000, http://www.waco93.com/Danforth -finalreport.pdf (accessed October 18, 2012).

3. Biography.com, "Jim Jones Biography," A&E Networks, http:// www.biography.com/people/jim-jones-10367607 (accessed October 18, 2012).

4. The Free Dictionary, s.v. "occult," http://www.thefreedictionary .com/occult (accessed October 19, 2012).

CHAPTER EIGHTEEN
VICTORY IN SURRENDER

1. John Dawson, *Taking Our Cities for God* (Lake Mary, FL: Charisma House, 2001), 2–4.

2. Sherman, *Spiritual Warfare for Every Christian*, 194. Viewed at Google Books.

3. Corrie ten Boom Museum, "History," http://www.corrietenboom. com/history.htm (accessed December 18, 2012).

4. F. Kefa Sempangi, *A Distant Grief* (Ventura, CA: Regal, 1979), 119–120.

5. Ibid, 126.

EMPOWERED
TO RADICALLY CHANGE
YOUR WORLD